BASEBALL'S
HOME
RUN
HITTERS
The Sultans of Swat

A publication of
Leisure Press.
597 Fifth Avenue: New York, N.Y. 10017

Library of Congress Cataloging in Publication Data

Nelson, Don.
  Baseball's home run hitters.

  Includes index.
  1. Batting (Baseball) 2. Baseball—United States—
History. 3. Baseball—United States Records. I. Title.
GV869.N45 1984 796.357'092'2 [B] 84-734
ISBN 0-88011-220-4

BASEBALL'S HOME RUN HITTERS

The Sultans of Swat

The Definitive Work on Home Runs and Home Run Hitters

Don Nelson

LEISURE PRESS

NEW YORK

CONTENTS

To my parents

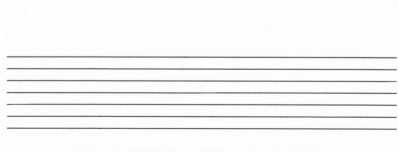

ACKNOWLEDGMENTS

This may be the most difficult section of the book to write, because so many people have helped me in so many ways, possibly without even knowing they were contributing.

My membership in the Society for American Baseball Research has been extremely beneficial. Several SABR members, starting with President Bob Davids, have been kind. I will mention especially Jerry Gregory, Bob McConnell, Fred Stein and John Thorn.

My primary data sources were the various SABR publications, especially the *Baseball Research Journals* and *This Date in Baseball History* all editions of the MacMillan *Baseball Encyclopedia* publications of *The Sporting News* and *The Sports Encyclopedia: Baseball* 5th Edition. The sports pages of the daily newspapers were also very helpful.

I thank Virginia Sandidge for yeoman typing assistance and Bill Carnahan and Debbie Shelton for graphics input. Finally, I thank my family for their understanding and encouragement.

THE BIG HIT

The home run is the most dramatic hit in baseball. What other event in a ball game is so thrilling as the announcer's voice, rising higher and higher and getting more and more excited, chanting, "It might be . . . it could be . . . it *is*! A Home Run!" or "There she goes . . . " or "Way back, way back . . . way back . . . " or "It's going . . . it's going . . . it's *gone*! A home run!"   It's undoubtedly the Big Hit. Why else do we and the sportscasters and writers have so many names for the same thing? Besides home run, we call it a homer, four-bagger, four-master, circuit clout (smash, blow, blast, etc.), round-tripper, four-base wallop (smash, blow, blast, etc.), the long ball . . . you add some more.

    We fans get into the act, too. We urge our favorites to hit the Big Hit: "Touch all the bases, Reggie!" "Knock it over the fence, Hank!" "Lose one, Stan!" "Park one, Willie!" "Bust one, Babe!" "Hit it out, Harm!" "Go for the distance, Mike!"   We say a player hits, hammers, pokes, parks, punches, smashes, slashes, crashes, bashes, swats, cracks, whacks, clouts, clubs, bangs, booms, raps, rips, drives, drills, slams, whams, bats, blasts, knocks, conks, strokes or sends the ball into the stands or otherwise connects for the distance.

We even have special names for special kinds of home runs (a grand slam which "clears the bases," an "inside-the-park homer," a "tape measure job"). What other event in a game, indeed, so consistently brings the throng to its feet, cheering, shouting, stomping, than the mighty home run? And why else do we give the muscled men who excel in hitting the long ball such a variety of virile names? ("long-ball hitter," "slugger," "walloper," "slammer," "thumper" and so on.)

Even if it isn't a bases-loaded job or a game-winner, every round-tripper is important because it always scores a run, and with only one swing of the bat. After all, scoring runs is the objective of the Grand Old Game.

The cracking bat, the soaring ball, the roaring crowd—that is the home run. That most thrilling of hits, the Big Hit, and the men who hit them, the Big Hitters, are the subjects of this book.

2

THE BIG HITTERS *

Is Ralph Kiner the seventh-leading home run hitter of all time? Is Mike Schmidt already ranked 13th? Is Babe Ruth still Number 1?

If career home runs is your measure of leading homer hitters, these ratings don't make sense, because Kiner is 27th, Schmidt 34th and Ruth second.

But career homers is not the only measure of a great long-ball hitter. Neither are yardsticks such as most-times-leading-league or consistency in hitting the long ball.

They're all good measures. And, taken altogether, career homers, league leaderships in four-baggers and number of big-output seasons measure a player's real homer-hitting ability.

---

*This chapter updated from an article by the same name and author in the 1982 *Baseball Research Journal*.

***RALPH KINER** is the seventh-leading **Big Hitter** of all time by the "N-Rating" system.*

That's why I use a system that ranks players as Big Hitters. It recognizes a player's ability to hit home runs over time and at points in time. It also measures leadership ability and tells how certain sluggers perform compared to other long ball hitters of their time and Big Hitters before or after their time. I call this ranking system the "Nelson rating" or "N-rating" for short.

Here is the "raw data" on five players:

	AARON	**RUTH**	**MAYS**	**KINER**	**SCHMIDT**
Career Homers	755(1st)	714(2d)	660(3d)	369(27th)	349(34th)
League Leads	4x	12xx	4	7xxx	5
30 Homer Seasons	7	2	5	2	6
40 +	8	7	4	3	2
50 +	—	3	2	2	—
60 +	—	1	—	—	—

x   — Including one tie
xx   — Including two ties
xxx   — Including three ties

Now here's how the "N-rating" works:

Major league players score one point for each 10 career home runs. Players pick up an additional 10 points each time they lead their league in home run production (5 for a tie). This is the leadership ingredient. (Even though nine National Leaguers walloped as many or more home runs as Tony Conigliaro in 1965, for instance, Tony is still rewarded for his American League dominance.)

The most difficult part of the calculation is big-output single seasons. Just what is an outstanding one-year performance? Well, if a pitcher wins 20 games or a batter averages .300 or drives in 100 runs, he's had a "great campaign" and is singled out for acclaim.

But what is the standard of excellence for a top home run year? 15? 25? 40? I set the standard at 30, because the man who slams 30 or more circuit clouts in a year has accomplished just as difficult a feat as the pitcher who twirls 20 wins.

Clearing the bases 30 or more times has the same degree of difficulty for a batter as winning 20 has for a pitcher. In the first 60 years of the Big Hitter era, from 1920 through 1979, there were 440, 20-wins-or-more season pitching performances. In the same span, there were virtually the same number of 30-or-more home run season performances, 444.

We have to start the comparison with 1920 because the home run really wasn't discovered until then. Twenty-game winners we have always had. But until Ruth cracked 54 long ones in 1920, nobody had hit even 30. Ruth's 29 round-trippers in 1919 for the Red Sox, when he was still occasionally pitching, were the most ever hit until then.

That's why I award 10 points every time a player hits 30 homers. Of those 444, 30-plus homer seasons, 318 were in the 30–39 category and 109 in the 40–49 range. With a degree of difficulty of about three, I figure 40–49 is worth 20 points. There have been 15, 50–59 performances (seven times more difficult to hit than 40), thus another 10 N-points are awarded. Finally, the two 60-homer campaigns by Babe Ruth and Roger Maris are 7.5 times more difficult than lofting 50, so 40 points are bestowed.

This rating system recognizes the exploits of the Conigliaros, the Colavitos and the Cashes, as well as the Mayses and Mantles.

Here, then, are the N-ratings of the five players charted earlier:

	AARON	**RUTH**	**MAYS**	**KINER**	**SCHMIDT**
Points for:					
Career Homers	75	71	66	36	34
League Leads	35	110	40	55	50
30 + Homers	70	20	50	20	60
40–49	160	140	80	60	40
50–59	—	90	60	60	—
60 +	—	40	—	—	—
	340(2d)	471 (1st)	296(3d)	231(7th)	1 84(13th)

Using this system, Ruth is the greatest Big Hitter in the game's history with 471 points. Aaron is second with 340 and a comfortable lead over Mays. Harmon Killebrew, Jimmie Foxx and Mickey Mantle come in fourth, fifth and sixth.

Hall of Famer Kiner (seventh) picks up a batrack full of points for league leaderships. Kiner was king in the National League from 1946 through 1952 as he won or tied for the league lead seven straight times. Not even Ruth can top this record of consecutive championships. So, though Kiner finished 124 behind Lou Gehrig as a career home run hitter (493 to 369), Ralph was a greater slugger in his time. Gehrig had tough competition for N-points in the likes of Babe Ruth, Hank Greenberg, Jimmie Foxx and Joe DiMaggio. Kiner at his best was challenged only by Johnny Mize. The top 10 is rounded off by Lou Gehrig, Eddie Mathews and Ernie Banks.

Some other interesting information the N-ratings reveal:

1. The preeminence of Ruth as the greatest Big Hitter is driven home. The Babe had more league leaderships in four-masters than any other player (10 outright, two ties), hit 50 or more round-trippers more times than anyone before or since (4) and hit 40 or more homers more years than anyone else (11). His seasonal high in home runs (60) stood for 34 years until Maris produced his 61 (in a longer season). His career homer record lasted even longer, 39 years, until Aaron hit his shot heard 'round the world (number 715 in 1974). I've already mentioned that the Sultan of Swat truly ushered in the age of the Big Hitter, a Golden Era that now stretches through more than 60 years of baseball.

2. In addition to Kiner and Schmidt, Hank Greenberg and Chuck Klein stand out as surprising long-ball blasters. Greenberg is 39th in career homers but 15th in the N-ratings. Klein is 47th career, 24th (tie) in N-points. Some who don't come up as high as their career totals might indicate are Stan Musial, Billy Williams and Al Kaline. All rate in the top 20 career, but fail to crack the top 25 "N." Reasons: only one league leadership among them, not that many big individual campaigns.

The Big Hitters: All Players with 100 or more "N" Points, through 1982.

1.	Babe Ruth*	471	17. *Reggie Jackson*	161
2.	Hank Aaron*	340	18. Duke Snider*	160
3.	Willie Mays*	296	19. *Willie Stargell*	147
4.	Harmon Killebrew	287	20. Rocky Colavito	142
5.	Jimmie Foxx*	278	21. Johnny Mize*	140
6.	Mickey Mantle*	243	22. Frank Howard	138
7.	Ralph Kiner*	231	23. Joe DiMaggio*	136
8.	Lou Gehrig*	224	24. Chuck Klein*	125
9.	Eddie Mathews*	211	Dick Allen	125
10.	Ernie Banks*	191	26. Gil Hodges	117
11.	Frank Robinson*	188	*Johnny Bench*	117
12.	Mel Ott*	186	28. Hack Wilson*	114
13.	*Mike Schmidt*	184	*Carl Yastrzemski*	114
14.	Ted Williams*	182	30. Stan Musial*	107
15.	Hank Greenberg*	178	Orlando Cepeda	107
16.	Willie McCovey	167	32. *George Foster*	106
			33. Hank Sauer	103
			34. Billy Williams	102
			Dave Kingman	102

*Half of the top six Big Hitters together. From left, **WILLIE MAYS (N-3)**, **MICKEY MANTLE (N-6), HANK AARON (N-2).** Courtesy Atlanta Braves*

3. Schmidt is the only active player with a good shot at the top 10. One more big year will catapult him into the 200-point range. It would take Reggie Jackson a minimum of two exceptionally big-hit seasons to pass Banks. But he'd then probably have to outdo Schmidt for the 10th spot. Mike has age on his side of the plate: he turned 33 in 1982. Reggie is three years older.

4. What about Roger Maris? Well, Rog chalked up a fat 56 points for his great 1961 effort, but closed his career with 97 points total, currently good for a two-way tie for 36th in the N-ratings.

5. "Home Run" Baker earned his nickname. The old "A" won three home run championships and tied for another. That's good for 35 points, most of them compiled in the "dead ball era" (1901–19). His 96 career homers gives him a grand total of 44. Gavvy Cravath, another early-day blaster, garners 55 points by the same route, and racks up 66 points overall. This makes him a greater long-ball hitter than Wally Berger, Yogi Berra and Joe Adcock. Baker, Cravath and Harry Davis (47 points) are the only pre-Ruthian names to show up in the top 100 of the N-ratings.

6. Harmon Killebrew is the only player in the top 12 "N" not in the Baseball Hall of Fame.

Others with 65 or more "N" Points:
Roger Maris 97, Norm Cash 97, Bobby Bonds 93, Rogers Hornsby 90, Ted Kluszewski 87, Cy Williams 85, *Gorman Thomas* 84, *Jim Rice* 83, Rudy York 77, Roy Campanella* 74, Ron Santo 74, Gus Zernial 73, Boog Powell 73, Roy Sievers 71, Al Rosen 69, Gavvy Cravath 66, *Tony Perez* 66, Larry Doby 65, *Lee May* 65.

The computations for these 54 Big Hitters and the other 47 players who comprise the top 101 Big Hitter list (made necessary by a tie for no. 100) appear in the Appendix.
(ACTIVE PLAYERS IN 1982 IN ITALIC)

*Hall of Fame member

3

30-HOMER HITTER = 20-GAME WINNER

When a pitcher wins 20 games in a season, he attracts headlines and a brisk trade in his bubblegum card. When a batter smacks 30 or more home runs, he may or may not enjoy the same recognition.

The story is told of Ralph Kiner seeking a raise after he led the league with 37 homers for the eighth-place Pirates in 1952. Branch Rickey gave him a pay cut, instead, explaining that "We could have finished last without you."

Every starting pitcher wants to win 20. All fans recognize the significance of the term "20-game winner." But who talks about a "30-homer hitter" with the same reverence?

The man who slams 30 or more circuit clouts in a year should get equal billing and the same trading card fame, though, because hitting 30 homers is just as difficult a feat as hurling 20 wins (virtually the same number of each performance in the 1920–79 period).

If anything, the 30-homer hitter should garner more acclaim, because a home run is essentially an individual accomplishment, while a 20-victory campaign is more a team achievement.

When a batter connects for a four-bagger, it's just him, the bat and the ball. When a pitcher wins a game, it's him, his fielders and his hitters. Other pitchers may even contribute to the "W." You can't win if you don't score and have some teammates around to catch the ball. Even if a pitcher should accomplish the incomparable by pitching a shutout, hitting a home run for the only run and striking out every batter, he would still need a catcher.

Early Wynn probably came closest to achieving the unassisted pitching victory. At age 39 and hurling for the pennant-bound White Sox in 1959, burly Early allowed only one hit and struck out 14 Red Sox. He also had a home run to drive in the only run and a double in the 1–0 whitewash. But he needed the help of his catcher to handle the strikes and his fielders for the other 13 putouts.

Twenty-game winners go with winning teams. 'Tain't necessarily so for 30-homer hitters. Consider Kiner. When he was leading the league (or tieing for it) seven straight years (1946–52) and hitting 30-plus homers for seven consecutive years (1947–53) he played on only one winning team. The '48 Pirates finished fourth that year, as Kiner tied for the league lead with 40 big pokes. Otherwise the Bucs were 7th-7th(tie)-6th-8th-7th and 8th through '52. During '53, when he lofted 35 round-trippers, he was traded from the (eventual) 8th-place Pirates to the 7th-place Cubs.

And how about all those years when those perennial also-rans, the Chicago Cubs, fielded a team of Ernie Banks and eight other guys? Ernie walloped 30 or more four-masters six times in the eight-year period 1955 through 1962 and never played for a winner. It wasn't until 1968 that Banks whacked 30 homers for an over-.500 club.

Banks never had a 20-win pitching teammate when he hit 30 or more homers for a team with a losing record. Kiner had one; Murry Dickson won 20 for the seventh-place Pirates in 1951.

Period	30-HR Performances			20-Win Performances		
	NL	AL	Total	NL	AL	Total
1920–29	13	16	29	43	47	90
1930–39	18	44	62	29	39	68
1940–49	17	22	39	28	27	55
1950–59	63	32	95	30	30	60
1960–69	62	55	117	43	30	73
1970–79	58	44	102	32	62	94
Totals	231	213	444	205	235	440

Note from the chart that 20-win pitching performances were more common in the 1920–49 period (213 W, 130 HR). Since then, it's been reversed (314 HR, 227 W), especially in the National League. So is a 30-homer campaign still the equivalent of a 20-win year? Let's compare a recent five-year period (the shortened 1981 season is excluded):

	30-HR Performances			20-Win Performances		
Year	**NL**	**AL**	**Total**	**NL**	**AL**	**Total**
1977	10	9	19	6	3	9
'78	3	7	10	2	6	8
'79	7	6	13	2	3	5
1980	3	6	9	2	5	7
'82	6	10	16	1	0	1
Totals	29	38	67	13	17	30

If the trend continues, it will take about a 35-homer season to be equivalent to a 20-W effort (there were 29, 35 or better homer performances in the five recent years listed).

But don't forget that individual effort of the Big Hitter!

BRONX BOMBERS IS RIGHT

Big Hitters have played a big role with the most successful team of the Century, the New York Yankees. From 1921 through 1981, the Yanks won 22 Series, 33 pennants and five division titles. No other team is even close to that record.

From 1920 through 1961, New York led the AL in home runs 30 times (two ties). Nineteen times when they paced the league in homers, it was accompanied by a pennant and 14 times by a world's championship. These accomplishments also leave all other teams out of the running for the near future.

From 1920 (when the Big Hitter era began) through 1982, the Bombers had 58, 30-or-better individual home run performances, 16 more than the next best team, the Boston—Milwaukee—Atlanta Braves. Four players—Ruth, Gehrig, DiMaggio and Mantle—supplied two-thirds of the Yankees' 58 big-output performances. The greatest homer-hitting pairs of team-mates in a single season have been two Yankee tandems, Maris-Mantle, 115 homers in 1961 and Ruth-Gehrig, 107 in 1927. In fact, these are the only two teams to have two players join up for more than 100 circuit

The greatest homer-hitting pair of teammates, ROGER MARIS (left) and MICKEY MANTLE (Yankees, 1961).

smashes in a season. Add Moose Skowron's 28 to the Maris-Mantle cannonade and Tony Lazzeri's 18 to the Ruth Gehrig avalanche and you instantly have the teams with most homers among three players, 143 for the '61 Yanks and 125 for the '27 New Yorkers.

Some have called the 1927 Yankees the greatest team in history. They won 110 games and swept the series as Ruth hit the fall classic's two (and only) homers.

The 1961 Gotham team won 109 games and cruised right on through the Series, wrecking the Reds four games to one. Those '61 belters also set the standard for team homers in a year—240. That group parked seven World Series homers. But the .105-batting Maris had only one of them and the injured Mantle none (in six at bats).

If that '61 pinstripe edition wasn't the greatest team in history, it certainly was the greatest homer-hitting team. Six, count 'em, six players poled 20 or more HR's. Besides Maris, Mantle and Skowron, they were: Yogi Berra 22, Elston Howard 21 and part-timer Johnny Blanchard 21.

Those two big blasters, Ruth and Gehrig, also sparked heavy-hitting Yankee teams on two other auspicious occasions. The Babe and Larrupin' Lou were "twin 40's," a rare feat, in both 1931 (46 each for 92 between them) and Ruth 49, Gehrig 41 for 90 as an entry in 1930. However, those were both years in which the Yankees lost the pennant to Connie Mack's Athletics! The A's were doing some pretty heavy homer work themselves in those days with Foxx and Al Simmons providing the heft.

The Yanks have not disappointed the power-hungry fan in World Series play, either. Consider these feats: Mantle leads all competitors with 18 Series swats, followed by Ruth with 15 and Yogi Berra with 12. They have 8 of the top 12 Series homer hitters (lifetime), although Reggie Jackson poled 2 of his 10 for the A's.

Jackson hit more in one Series regardless of length than anybody else. He had five, including three in the sixth and final game in the '77 classic. The only other three-in-a-game mauler in Series history was Ruth, who turned the trick in both the 1926 and 1928 Series.

And how about the grandest home run of any type, the kind unloaded with the bases jammed? The Yanks have the majority of those in Series play, too, 7 out of 12, hit by Tony Lazzeri ('36), Gil McDougald ('51), Mickey Mantle ('53), Yogi Berra and Moose Skowron ('56), Bobby Richardson ('60) and Joe Pepitone ('64).

Finally, the New Yorkers smashed more HR than any team in a Series of any length, 12 in the victorious seven-game set with the Dodgers in 1956.

If the Yankees have consistently had big bats in their lineup, deserving of the nickname Bronx Bombers, the Chicago White Sox have earned the nickname Hitless Wonders. The 06 South Siders were first so-tagged. All

Team Big Hitter (30 or more HR) Performances, 1920–82, with first and latest team BH, year accomplished and number hit.

Team	No.	First	Latest
Yankees	58	'20 — Babe Ruth 54x	'82 — Dave Winfield 37
Braves	42	'30 — Wally Berger 38	'82 — Dale Murphy 36, Bob Horner 32
Giants	40	'29 — Mel Ott 42	'73 — Bobby Bonds 39
Red Sox	35	'36 — Jimmie Foxx 41	'82 — Dwight Evans 32
Cubs	32	'27 — Hack Wilson 30xx	'79 — Dave Kingman 48x
Reds	30	'38 — Ival Goodman 30	'79 — George Foster 30
Phils	29	'23 — Cy Williams 41x	'82 — Mike Schmidt 35
A's	26	'22 — Tilly Walker 37	'80 — Tony Armas 35
Dodgers	25	'30 — Babe Herman 35	'82 — Pedro Guerrero 32
Tigers	22	'35 — Hank Greenberg 36xx	'82 — Lance Parrish 32
Indians	20	'31 — Earl Averill 32	'82 — Andre Thornton 32
Senators—Twins	19	'57 — Roy Sievers 42x	'70 — Harmon Killebrew 41
Pirates	17	'47 — Ralph Kiner 51xx	'82 — Jason Thompson 31
Browns—Orioles	16	'22 — Ken Williams 39x	'82 — Eddie Murray 32
Cardinals	14	'22 — Rogers Hornsby 42x	'70 — Richie Allen 34
Pilots—Brewers	10	'70 — Tommy Harper 31	'82 — Gorman Thomas 39xx, Ben Oglivie 34, Cecil Cooper 32
(New) Senators—Rangers	7	'67 — Frank Howard 36	'78 — Bobby Bonds 31 +
Angels	8	'62 — Leon Wagner 37	'82 — Reggie Jackson 39xx, Doug DeCinces 30
White Sox	6	'70 — Bill Melton 33	'77 — Oscar Gamble 31, Richie Zisk 30
Mets	4	'62 — Frank Thomas 34	'82 — Dave Kingman 37x
Expos	3	'70 — Rusty Staub 30	'79 — Larry Parrish 30
Padres	3	'70 — Nate Colbert 38	'79 — Dave Winfield 34
Colt .45s—Astros	2	'67 — Jimmy Wynn 37	'69 — Jimmy Wynn 33
Royals	1	'75 — John Mayberry 34	'75 — John Mayberry 34
Blue Jays	1	'80 — John Mayberry 30	'80 — John Mayberry 30
Mariners	0		
	470		

x — League Lead
xx — Tied for League Lead
+ — Hit 2 for White Sox, 29 for Rangers

Note that John Mayberry has been the first and only Big Hitter for two different expansion teams and Jimmy Wynn the only one for the Astros. Also, Bobby Bonds, Dave Kingman and Dave Winfield have been the most recent BH for two teams each, the Mets and Cubs for Kingman, the Giants and Rangers for Bonds and the Padres and Yankees for Winfield.

***BILL MELTON** was a triple hero for the White Sox.*
Courtesy Chicago White Sox

the Sox batters combined for seven homers in 1906, dropped to five in 1907, pinged a mere three in 1908 and a paltry four in 1909. From 1905 through 1910 they managed 37 home runs, about six a year. But every "Pale Hose" club from 1901 through 1969 could just as well have been called Hitters Wonders, at least as far as Big Hitters is concerned.

The 1970 campaign was the first that any Chicago American club could boast of a Big Hitter. The Sox' perennial quest for a long-ball hitter ended in that year as Bill Melton hoisted 33 over the fence. Alas, the White Sox should have stuck to their tried-and-true good field, no hit, grind-it-out format: they had the worst record in the majors that season!

The White Sox did well in the pre-Big Hitter Era when it really didn't matter if you could hit home runs or not. They won four flags with their plinkety-plink attack between 1901 and 1919 and two out of the three World Series they participated in (the Series they lost was the infamous Black Sox scandal of 1919). But the Sox have won only one pennant since, in 1959. After the long search for a long ball hitter ended in 1970, they produced six BH performances in eight years, including three league-leading efforts (Melton 33 in '71 and Richie Allen 37 in '72 and 32 in '74). But the team could do no better than second in its division in that 1970–77 span.

Melton emerges as a triple hero: first in a White Sox suit to hit 30-plus big hits, first in that garb to lead the league and the all-time record holder for home runs with that team (154).

But to draw the contrast between the Yanks and the Sox, the Bombers have 17 players with more home runs as a Yankee than Melton had with the Sox.

Team Leaders in HR, through 1982:

Braves, Hank Aaron	733	A's, Jimmie Foxx	302
Yankees, Babe Ruth	659	(New) Senators-Rangers,	
Giants, Willie Mays	646	Frank Howard	246
Senators-Twins,		Indians, Earl Averill	226
Harmon Killebrew	559	Astros, Jimmy Wynn	223
Red Sox, Ted Williams	521	Brewers, *Gorman Thomas*	197
Cubs, Ernie Banks	512	Royals, *Amos Otis*	178
Cardinals, Stan Musial	475	Expos, *Gary Carter*	171
Pirates, Willie Stargell	475	Padres, Nate Colbert	163
Dodgers, Duke Snider	389	White Sox, Bill Melton	154
Reds, *Johnny Bench*	377	Mets, *Dave Kingman*	141
Tigers, Norm Cash	373	Angels, Don Baylor	117
Phils, *Mike Schmidt*	349	Blue Jays, John Mayberry	92
Browns-Orioles, Boog Powell	303	Mariners, Dan Meyer	64

ITALIC—STILL ACTIVE WITH TEAM AT START OF 1983 SEASON

5

YEARS OF THE BIG BATS

Babe Ruth practically invented the home run, then apparently kept the art and science of hitting it a secret through most of the Roaring '20's. Well, maybe he shared some tips with his teammate, Lou Gehrig. There were never more than four Big Hitter performances in any season from 1920 through 1928 and only 19 total in those nine years. Ruth's name was on eight of them.

But in 1929, it is sometimes alleged that somebody put a bunny in the ball and suddenly, there were a lot of fast learners. There were 10 BH performances in '29 and just as many in 1930, more in two years than in the previous nine.

In some ways, these crash-to-depression years were the most amazing of all big bat seasons in the history of the sport, especially in the Senior Circuit.

It was in 1930 that Hack Wilson set his still-standing NL record of 56 home runs. That record has been approached in the intervening years by Ralph Kiner, Johnny Mize, Willie Mays and George Foster, but never matched. Hack had his second-best career total, 39, the year before, but that was only fourth best in the league.

Mel Ott, number 12 in the N-ratings, had his greatest home run season in 1929, with 42. Yet, even though Mel was destined to lead or tie for the league leadership in circuit smashes six times in the future, this, the only year in which he cracked 40 or more, was not enough to win the championship.

The 1929 homer title fell instead to Chuck Klein, who conked 43. Klein had his second-best year the next season, 1930, with 40, but this time it was he who had to play second fiddle to Wilson's 56. Klein, also, never hit so many as 40 again.

Rogers Hornsby hit 39 in 1929, matching his next-to-best performance, and the last time the Rajah played more than 100 games in a season. These four, Wilson, Ott, Klein and Hornsby, dominated the long ball hitting in the National League for 20 years, garnering 16 home run championships, or ties for the top, in the '20s, '30s and in 1942 (when Ott led).

After the 1929–30 homer splurge in the National League, somebody or something apparently let the "lively" out of the ball, however. There were never as many as 10 individual Big Hitter performances, that is 30 or more round-trippers by a player in a season, for the next 20 years. In 1950, the barrier was broken as 11 men touched off 30 or more fence-clearing rockets in the two leagues combined. But the magic just wouldn't come back. The majors could produce only 6 to 12 BH performances for another 10 years (1951–60).

Apparently the old horsehide was about as resilient as the manufacturers could stuff, wind and sew it, so the major moguls found a new way to increase the BH output; they trotted out more teams.

The AL put up two new entries for 1961 and immediately Roger Maris responded by shattering Ruth's record and 12 others joined him as Big Hitters. Besides Maris, five other ALers had tremendous seasons, four of them attaining personal highs in that expansion year, to wit: Mickey Mantle 54, Jim Gentile 46, Rocky Colavito 45 and Norm Cash 41. The other one, Harmon Killebrew, mashed 46, a big year, but not his best (he whopped 49 on two occasions).

Seeing this, the NL got into the act in '62 and added two new teams of its own. And, what do you know! There were 14 BH performances in the majors.

But, wouldn't you know it, parity started to creep in again and the supply of BH performances dwindled back to '30s and '40s levels. There were only seven in 1968 and strikeouts were rampant around home plate.

Solution: still more teams. The '69 expansion to 12 teams in each league got the BH total up to 16 and 19 in '70.

But, curses, the Big Hitter breed was again on the verge of extinction, as only four players stroked 30 or more HRs in '74 and again in '76. The AL

HARMON KILLEBREW, among others, had a Big Hitter year in 1961.

once more was the circuit to seize the initiative, add teams and up output. Two new clubs were created and Big Hitters again shattered the air with their mighty blows. The 1970 total of 19 was matched in '77.

This is all a little facetious, of course. But the addition of teams suspiciously coincides with big-output seasons, particularly in the American League. The alleged "lively ball" brought out the best in the National's big blasters in '29–'30.

Another event impacted on the '40s: World War II. Those war years, as we might expect, could be called the Years of the Light Bats. When Ted Williams sailed 36 into the seats in 1942 (before he flew off to battle), this accomplishment was enough to win the championship in the American League. It was also the most homers hit by a major league player for the duration of those lean years. Four players won crowns by hitting less than 30 home runs from 1942 through 1945. Nick Etten's 22 long pokes in 1944 were enough to put his name in the record book.

Four players tied for the AL lead with the same 22 total in 1981, but that was in a strike-shortened year.

6

DR. LONGBALL: SURE CURE?

Imagine a general manager watching a commercial. A strapping chap in a white coat says: "Hitting more, but scoring less? Is that what's bugging you, bub? Call me, Dr. Longball. I'll put punch in your attack."

So, how about it? Can Dr. Longball cure anything that may ail a club? Can a team be built and managed around a home run strategy? Or is it only a useful tactic which nobody can prescribe?

Let's take a look at the patients' charts for a prescription.

The Brewers rode the long ball to a pennant in 1982, but got their come-uppance from the speedy, sharp-hitting Cardinals in the World Series. It was strictly David (Cards 67 season homers, low in both leagues) against Goliath (Brewers 216 season four-baggers, tops in both circuits and sixth on the all-time list).

That wasn't the first time the worst power-hitting team in the major leagues had won a pennant and Series on pitching, speed and defense. The 1924 Senators boffed a mere 22 during the season, the most miserable in both leagues, yet put a plague on the Giants in the fall classic.

However, both the '82 Redbirds and '24 Senators did not disdain Dr. Longball as a pick-me-up in October. The Cards muscled four out as they edged the Milwaukee maulers in seven games (the Brewers hit five HR). The Senators parked five long swats (all by Goose Goslin and Bucky Harris) to give the Giants an indigestible dose of defeat (the Giants, meanwhile, had four long balls in their dying effort) also in seven games.

Two other teams didn't swallow the HR pill with any regularity, yet had robust records. The '65 Dodgers were last in the majors in long bombs (78), but in the World Series whipped up on the Twins, who had belted almost twice as many, 150, in the regular season. The '59 White Sox picked up a pennant despite ordinary home run numbers (97, last in both leagues); however, the Dodgers took them in the Series. Ted Kluszewski cracked three HR in a losing cause for the Sox.

But other clubs have found health and happiness by dosing their opponents with bad medicine in the form of home runs.

During the Big Hitter era, 1920–82, 45 teams led their league in HR and simultaneously captured the flag. Of these 45, 26 went on to win the World Series.

In strictly head-to-head matchups, regardless of league HR leaderships, the team which had hit the most homers coming into the Series defeated the team with fewer clouts, 36 out of 63 times, a 57 percent majority.

Power was more preeminent in the earlier years of the BH era. From 1920 through 1959, the heavier homer-hitting team at season's end won 26 world titles (65 percent) to 14 for the less powerful squad. From 1960 through 1982, the lighter-hitting nines have been coming through more often in the Series (13 to 10 or 56.5 percent).

Leaving the regular season aside and isolating Series performances, the team which does the best job of reaching the seats in the championships most frequently inflicts more pain than it endures. In the 63 Series under scrutiny, the outfit with the most home runs during the autumn battle has won 54 percent of the time. However, there is a trend away from power as the way to go to win:

	1920–59	1960–82	Total
Team with most HR wins Series	25	9	34
Each team same number HR	6	3	9
Team with most HR loses Series	9	11	20
Total	40	23	63

No winning team has out-homered the opposition in a World Series since the '76 Reds. In 1981, the Dodgers and Yankees each biffed six; otherwise Dr. Longball was not operating so well in the other five face-offs.

The 1936–39 Yankees were the great dominators when it came to sickening their opponents with a steady diet of long balls. Their regular season HR totals buried their various NL October opponents by 696–371 in the four years. In the four Series (they won them all), the margin was 23–7 over their assorted NL patsies. The great 1949–53 New Yorkers won five straight Series, but by that time they were playing a little different game. The Nationals out-hammered them by a collective 817–682 coming off the regular seasons. But at Series time, the Bronx Bombers reverted to their accustomed masher role, clubbing 28 to the Nationals' 20.

The Yankees murdered the American League in the 12-year period 1936–47. They led the league in HR every season in that span, winning eight pennants and seven Series. The Dodgers (Brooklyn-type) were lethal with their big bats from 1949 through 1955 (counting a 1954 tie with the Giants for the HR leadership). In those seven seasons, they finished first in the standings four times, but managed to defeat the Yankees in Series play only in the final year of the skein. The Dodgers (LA-type) also dominated the NL long-ball hitting contests from 1977 through '81. In that streak, they gathered up three pennants and likewise were successful against the Yanks in only the final try in '81.

When the Yanks and Dodgers tangle in post-season competition, you can bet your stethoscope that Dr. Longball will be getting a lot of calls.

Through the Big Hitter years, the Cardinals, on the other hand, have been the leading exponents on how to beat the other team every which way you can, but, in almost all cases, not with home run cuts. The Gateway team has been in 13 Series between 1926 and 1982 and won nine of them. Yet they out-homered their October nemeses only once; in '44 they drove three out to the Brownies' one. They did manage to match the HR totals of the Yankees, Tigers and Yankees again in '26, '34 and '43, respectively. For the 13 Series, they are down 35–65 in HR, but up 9–4 in the result that really counts.

As far as those teams turning in really heavy homer years (in excess of 200), they have had mixed success:

Year-Team		No. HR/Rank	Team Finish
1961	Yankees	240/1	World Champion
1963	Twins	225/2	Third
1947	Giants (NY)	221/3	Fourth
1956	Reds	221/3	Third
1964	Twins	221 /3	Seventh
1982	Brewers	216/6	AL Champion
1977	Red Sox	213/7	Second (tie)—AL East
1962	Tigers	209/8	Fourth
1953	Dodgers	208/9	NL Champion
1966	Braves	207/10	Fifth
1973	Braves	206/11	Fifth—NL West
1962	Giants (SF)	204/12	NL Champion
1970	Red Sox	203/13	Third—AL East
1980	Brewers	203/13	Third—AL East
1955	Dodgers	201/15	World Champion

The 1947 Giants were the first team to hit more than 200 HR in a season. The Yankees hold the single-season record but had a really big year only that one time and they have not led the league in home runs since their big year (1961). Six franchises have had 200-plus homer campaigns two different times. No two teams in the same league have ever hit more than 200 round-trippers in the same year.

So, when the call comes for Dr. Longball, should a team answer? I believe a good injection of umph by the good doctor will more often than not promote health and well being in the ball park. Take speed if you please; like PacMan, the best strategy would seem to be to gulp those power pills and eat up the opposition.

7

THAT WAS A WEEK THAT WAS

When pitcher Clay Bryant hit a grand slam in the 10th inning of a game in 1937 to win one for the Cubbies, it was unusual for two reasons: he was pitching in relief of Charlie Root, who had homered earlier in the game and it was the only time a pitcher ever hit the four-run jackpot beyond regulation.

The people who witnessed that event could count themselves among the chosen few to see such a unique home run. But what chance does the ordinary fan have to see an extraordinary home run like Bryant's, or even one only a little out of the ordinary—say a grand slam, game-winning, extra-inning blow or one delivered by a pinch hitter or a pitcher? For that matter, what are the chances on any given day of seeing any kind of a home run?

To test that out, I kept a log of all games and all homers hit for one week early in May, 1983 without knowing in advance what kind of week it might be.

CLAY BRYANT, *the only pitcher to hit the four-run jackpot in extra innings (Cubs, 1937).*

George Brace Photo

Here's what this average kind of week produced for the average kind of spectators who went out to the park or watched or listened to the games played that week that was, Tuesday, May 3 through Monday, May 9:

You could have picked almost any of the 73 games and been assured of seeing at least one four-bagger. Sixty-three games or 86 percent had one home run or more. Most often you would have seen one home run (37 percent of all games) or two (33 percent). You wouldn't have been so sure of seeing your favorite team or player connect. But the home team did homer 62 percent of the time.

There was a total of 120 big blows, an average of 1.6 per game. Of the 690 runs scored, 192 or 28 percent, rode home because of home runs. Most were hit with the bases empty as illustrated by the 1.6 runs per home run average.

As for home runs a little out of the ordinary (I would classify none of the 120 "extraordinary"), here's what happened: one grand slam; six three-run productions; three in extra innings; three by pinch hitters and none by a pitcher. There were no inside-the-park jobs. Four different players hit two in one game. Twice there were two consecutive long swats. Twenty-eight players hit their first home run of the season during those seven days in May.

Here's a present-tense recap of home run highlights in a week that was:

Tuesday—At least one home run is hit in each of the 12 games played. Dwight Evans' three-run homer makes the Red Sox 3–1 winners over the A's in Boston. Mike Schmidt busts his seventh of the season, tieing him with Dale Murphy of the Braves for the league lead, as the Phils demolish the Reds 13–7 at home.

Wednesday—Pedro Guerrero of the Dodgers also ties for the league leadership with his seventh big blow of the campaign; more significantly, the long hit is in the bottom of the ninth at Dodger Stadium and hands the Angelenos a 3–2 win over the Pirates.

Doug DeCinces, meanwhile, takes over the AL lead with his seventh and eighth blows in a game in which DeCinces' Angels measure the Orioles in Baltimore, 16–8.

Elsewhere in the AL, opposing shortstops both take balls the distance. The Tigers' Alan Trammell lofts his first of the year and the Mariners' Todd Cruz cracks his fifth. Trammell bats ninth in the Tigers' order, Cruz eighth in the Mariners' lineup. The final score is 5–1 in favor of the Mariners in Seattle. Back in the National in San Diego, the Padres crush the defending World Champion Cardinals 10–0 without benefit of any HR.

Thursday—It's a light schedule, with only three games played. The one homer of note is bashed by Dale Murphy of the Braves. It's his eighth of the year, good for the league lead and helps the Braves take the Astros 6–3 in Atlanta.

Hitless Wonders no more, the White Sox were divisional champions in 1983. Super rookie RON KITTLE'S power hitting (35 HR, 100 RBI) was one of the reasons for the Sox's success.

Courtesy Chicago White Sox

Friday—In the "Game of the Week" for HR thrills, the Mets keep battling from behind, hit four, two-out homers for all seven of their runs. In a 3 1/2-hour, 13-inning struggle, the Shea Stadium tenants finally whip the Reds. Trailing 3–0 in the eighth, Danny Heep socks a pinch homer to bring the Mets up to 3–1. Dave Kingman's two-run blast in the bottom of the ninth, his fifth of the year, lifts the Mets into a tie and sends the game into extra innings. Gary Redus, who hit his fifth fourth-bagger of the young season earlier, triples for the Reds in the top of the 10th and jogs home on Eddie Milner's double to put the Reds back on top, 4–3. But Hubie Brooks' shot in the last of the 10th ties it again. Finally, George Foster's three-run homer in the 13th ends it, 7–4 Mets.

In other NL games, Tony Perez' three-run HR in the top of the ninth wins one for the Phillies, 5–2, over the homestanding Expos; Jack Clark's two-run production in the sixth makes the Giants 2–1 winners over the Pirates in San Francisco and Keith Moreland's two-run HR in the first inning is the eventual margin for the Cubs as they edge the Padres, 3–2, in San Diego. Farther up the West Coast, the Dodgers lambaste the Cardinals 16–10; Ken Landreaux and Dusty Baker touch all the bases in Chavez Ravine.

Over in the American, there are three out-of-the-ordinary home run performances. Cal Ripken lofts two in Baltimore as the Orioles romp over the A's, 9–2, and Gorman Thomas sends one into the seats with two teammates aboard in Milwaukee. Alas, the other Brewers don't hit much and the pitching doesn't hold up as the defending AL Champion Brewers succumb to the Rangers, 9–4. Steve Kemp and Lou Piniella hit consecutive homers in the Yankees' 8–4 win over the Twins in the Minnesota Metrodome.

Saturday—The homer of the day and of the week jumps off Tony Armas' bat in Boston. Armas, the designated hitter and his Red Sox mates smother the Indians 8–0, with half the runs coming around on Tony's grand slam.

The remaining AL roundup: Doug DeCinces adds to his league lead with his ninth four-bagger of the year and Daryl Sconiers delivers a pinch-hit blast as the Angels edge the Tigers in Detroit, 6–5; Lou Whitaker delivers his second homer in two days and likewise his second of the year leading off the game in the losing cause. Willie Upshaw of the Blue Jays smacks a three-run homer in Toronto as the Canadian team prevails over the Royals, 7–4; George Brett, batting well over .400 and hitting safely in his 18th consecutive game, knocks in all of KC's runs with two-run and one-run homers and a single.

Roy Smalley of the Yankees sends a ball into the stands with a runner aboard in the first inning in Minnesota; Dave Winfield's ball also finds the seats for two in a row. It's also the second day in a row that Yankee batters deliver consecutive blasts. The Yanks go on to beat the Twins 8–7 on Rick Cerone's three-run clout in the eighth, which climaxes a five-run inning and unknots a 5–5 tie.

In the NL, Mike Jorgensen clips a two-run, pinch-hit homer, his first of the year, for the Mets in the bottom of the ninth, but it's too little and too late as the Reds triumph in Shea, 7–5. Bob Horner unloads his seventh circuit smash of the year in Atlanta as the Braves crush the Astros 10–1.

Ron Cey clubs his first home run of the season for his new team, the Cubs, but not within the friendly confines of Wrigley Field. Cey's first four-bagger, coming a month into the season, helps hoist the Cubs to a 6–4 win over the Padres in San Diego. Cey connected for 24 homers in the 1982 season with his former team, the Dodgers.

Sunday—Once again, no matter which of the 12 games you might have chosen to watch, you would have seen at least one home run hit. Of the 24 contesting teams (there is one rainout), 17 hit home runs. Nine of the 12 home teams homer.

Seven players put on their Sunday best by slugging their maiden homers on this day in May.

The American League feature is Robin Yount's three-run, bottom-of-the-ninth round-tripper which makes the Brewers 6–3 victors over the Rangers. The A's and O's tough it out through four rain delays in Baltimore with Wayne Gross' home run the only action around home plate as the A's win it, 1–0. George Brett keeps his 19-game hitting streak going with a two-run clout, his eighth of the year, as the Royals beat the Blue Jays in Toronto, 6–1.

In the Senior Circuit, Darrell Evans drills two-run and three-run homers, his fifth and sixth, to help the Giants bury the Pirates in the City by the Bay, 12–1. Veteran Dusty Baker and rookie Greg Brock each hit solo homers, each their fifth of the campaign, to spur the Dodgers on to a three-game sweep of the Cardinals in Southern California. The final score is 6–4.

Monday—Is it possible that major league players suffer from the Monday blahs just like a lot of the rest of us? Oh, sure, there are 13 homers hit in eight games (two HR in six games, one in another and none in the eighth). But none of them is anything to write home about. Well, maybe Greg Brock can say, "Look, Ma, I hit my sixth." Or Carlton Fisk can say, "I finally got one." But none is particularly dramatic or unusual.

So, maybe you'll never witness a four-bagger the likes of the one Clay Bryant hit back in '37. Maybe nobody ever will again. But it could happen. Like the man said, "Baseball is a funny game."

8

FOUR MASTERS, TERRIFIC TRIOS AND DYNAMIC DUOS

Only one team in major league history had four players hit 30 or more home runs in the same season. Name the year, the team and the Four Masters who did it. (See end of chapter for answer.)

Only one team had two players hit 50 or more homers in a year. That Dynamic Duo has been discussed previously and is also listed at the end of this chapter.

In addition to these special accomplishments, 18 teams have had three players who hit 30 or more HR in a year and there have been 10 other occurrences of two players hitting 40 or more.

Only one team ever had three players hit 40 or more four-baggers. Identify the year, team and Terrific Trio. (See end of chapter for this answer also.)

The Tri-Thirties:

PHILS '29:		YANKEES '41:		GIANTS '47:	
Chuck Klein	43x	Charlie Keller	33	Johnny Mize	51xx
Lefty O'Doul	32	Tommy Henrich	31	Willard Marshall	36
Don Hurst	31	Joe DiMaggio	30	Walker Cooper	35
	106		94		122

DODGERS '50:		DODGERS '53:		REDS '56:	
Gil Hodges	32	Duke Snider	42	Frank Robinson	38
Duke Snider	31	Roy Campanella	41	Wally Post	36
Roy Campanella	31	Gil Hodges	31	Ted Kluszewski	35
	94		114		109

SENATORS '59:		BRAVES '61:		GIANTS '63:	
Harmon Killebrew	42xx	Joe Adcock	35	Willie McCovey	44xx
Jim Lemon	33	Hank Aaron	34	Willie Mays	38
Bob Allison	30	Eddie Mathews	32	Orlando Cepeda	34
	105		101		116

TWINS '63:		GIANTS '64:		TWINS '64:	
Harmon Killebrew	45x	Willie Mays	47x	Harmon Killebrew	49x
Bob Allison	35	Orlando Cepeda	31	Bob Allison	32
Jimmie Hall	33	Jim Hart	31	Tony Oliva	32
	113		109		113

BRAVES '65:		BRAVES '66:		GIANTS '66:	
Eddie Mathews	32	Hank Aaron	44x	Willie Mays	37
Hank Aaron	32	Joe Torre	36	Willie McCovey	36
Mack Jones	31	Felipe Alou	31	Jim Hart	33
	95		111		106

REDS '70:		RED SOX '77:		BREWERS '82:	
Johnny Bench	45x	Jim Rice	39x	Gorman Thomas	39xx
Tony Perez	40	George Scott	33	Ben Oglivie	34
Lee May	34	Butch Hobson	30	Cecil Cooper	32
	119		102		105

x — League Leader
xx — Tied for Lead

Note that the Giants and Twins had successive Tri-30's in 1963–64. And the Braves turned the Tri-30 trick two years in a row (1965–66). Aaron, the game's all-time homer leader in terms of career clouts, was on four different Braves 30+ combos, in 1961, '65, '66 and '73. The only trio to make a repeat performance was the Dodger threesome of Hodges, Snider and Campanella in 1950 and again in '53.

The Twin Forties:

YANKEES '27:		YANKEES '30:		YANKEES '31:	
Babe Ruth	60x	Babe Ruth	49x	Babe Ruth	46xx
Lou Gehrig	47	Lou Gehrig	41	Lou Gehrig	46xx
	107		90		92

DODGERS '53:		DODGERS '54:		REDS '55:	
Duke Snider	42	Gil Hodges	42	Ted Kluszewski	47x
Roy Campanella	41	Duke Snider	40	Wally Post	40
	83 +		82		87 + +

TIGERS '61:		GIANTS '61:		RED SOX '69:	
Rocky Colavito	45	Orlando Cepeda	46x	Carl Yastrzemski	40
Norm Cash	41	Willie Mays	40	Rico Petrocelli	40
	86		86		80

REDS '70:	
Johnny Bench	45
Tony Perez	40
	85 +

x	— League Leader
xx	— Tied for Lead
+	— Also part of a Trio-30 group
+ +	— This is *not* the National League record for most HR by two players on the same team in a year. Hack Wilson's 56 and Gabby Hartnett's 37 set the record of 93 with the 1930 Chicago Cubs.

Hank Aaron's name, like Ruth's, pops up over and over whenever the home run is the subject. He teamed with Braves bammer Eddie Mathews to form the top homer-hitting pair on one team over an extended period. In the 13 years when these two were both in the same uniform (1954 through 1966), they knocked 863 baseballs out of sight.

Aaron and Mathews once hit home runs on two consecutive pitches, not so remarkable; but when Wes Covington hit the third straight pitch for the third homer in a row, that was something.

The second-best partnership was the Ruth-Gehrig duo. These two fell four short of the Aaron-Mathews barrage while both were Yankees at the same time, from 1923 through 1934:

AARON–MATHEWS, BRAVES				Total	RUTH–GEHRIG, YANKEES				Total
1954	13 +	40	=	53	1923	41x +	1	=	42
1955	27 +	41	=	68	1924	46x +	0	=	46
1956	26 +	37	=	63	1925	25 +	20	=	45
1957	44x +	32	=	76	1926	47 +	16	=	63
1958	30 +	31	=	61	1927	60x +	47	=	107
1959	39 +	46x	=	85	1928	54x +	27	=	81
1960	40 +	39	=	79	1929	46x +	35	=	81
1961	34 +	32	=	66	1930	49x +	41	=	90
1962	45 +	29	=	74	1931	46xx +	46 xx	=	92
1963	44xx +	23	=	67	1932	41 +	34	=	75
1964	24 +	23	=	47	1933	34 +	32	=	66
1965	32 +	32	=	64	1934	22 +	49x	=	71
1966 +	44 +	16	=	60					
13 yrs	442 +	421	=	863	12 yrs	511 +	348	=	859
Avg./Yr.	34 +	32.4	=	66.4	Av g./Yr.	42.6 +	29	=	71.6

x — League Leader
xx — Tied for Lead
+ — Milwaukee Braves became Atlanta Braves

Note that Gehrig out-muscled Ruth only once, in 1934, the year before the Bambino turned 40 and finished his career with the Boston Braves. And, oddly enough, Aaron and Mathews were never "Twin 40s."

There are four combos with credentials for the best homer-hitting trio on one club over an extended period. The group that stayed together the longest and hit the most home runs was the Billy Williams-Ron Santo-Ernie Banks threesome. They teamed for 903 circuit blows with the Cubs over 12 years, 1960–71. This triumvirate was remarkable for the equality of its members. They were less than three HR apart on an average-per-year basis (see chart). However, their combined homers-per-season average fell far short of the other three top triple threats.

Babe Ruth, Lou Gehrig and Tony Lazzeri smashed an average of 95 home runs a year among them when all played for the Yankees in the nine-year period 1926–34. This is almost 20 big hits a year better than the Cub boppers, who had an average of about 75. The detracting part of the long-run Murderers Row performance is that the show's star, Ruth, contributed more than three times as many long swats as Lazzeri, the bit player.

The three-sided Dodger triangle of Duke Snider, Gil Hodges and Roy Campanella creamed one more ball than the Yankee bangers (855–854), but took one more year to do it. These Big Hitters were simultaneously teammates for the Brooklyn version of the Dodgers for 10 years, from 1948 through 1957. The per-year average of the Bums' bashers was 85.5, nearly 10 less than the Yankees' crackers, but 10 more than the Cubs' conkers.

The fourth three-man force of interest was the Hank Aaron-Eddie Mathews-Joe Adcock assault group which accounted for 846 homers over nine years, 1954–62 for the Milwaukee Braves, an average of 94 a year, one short of the men of the Yankees group.

Frank Thomas followed Mathews, Aaron and Adcock in the batting order one day and the four of them made a contribution to baseball lore by clubbing four consecutive home runs.

Campanella's tragic disabling accident following the '57 season (and preceding the team's move to the West Coast) broke up the long run of the Dodger show; Adcock's trade to the Indians ended the Braves affiliation; Ruth's release to the Braves terminated the Yankee troupe's performance; Banks' retirement ended the 12-year run of the Cub clubbers.

The comparisons of these outstanding outfits:

CUBS, 1960–1971	No. HR	Avg./Yr.
Billy Williams	319	26.6
Ron Santo	300	25
Ernie Banks	284	23.7
12 yrs.	903	75.25

DODGERS, 1948–1957	No. HR	Avg./Yr.
Duke Snider	316	31.6
Gil Hodges	297	29.7
Roy Campanella	242	24.2
10 yrs.	855	85.5

YANKEES, 1926–1934		
Babe Ruth	399	44.3
Lou Gehrig	327	36.3
Tony Lazzeri	128	14.2
9 Yrs.	854	94.9

BRAVES, 1954–1962		
Eddie Mathews	327	36.3
Hank Aaron	298	33.1
Joe Adcock	221	24.5
9 Yrs.	846	94

THE FOUR MASTERS

DODGERS '77:	
Steve Garvey	33
Reggie Smith	32
Dusty Baker	30
Ron Cey	30
Total	125

THE TERRIFIC TRIO

BRAVES '73:	
Dave Johnson	43
Darrell Evans	41
Hank Aaron	40
Total	124

THE DYNAMIC DUO

YANKEES '61:	
Roger Maris	61
Mickey Mantle	54
Total	115

The "Four Masters," from left, STEVE GARVEY, DUSTY BAKER, RON CEY and REGGIE SMITH (Dodgers, 1977).

Courtesy Los Angeles Dodgers

Only one of the Four Masters, Reggie Smith, ever hit 30 or more in a year any other time (he had 30 in '71 with the Red Sox). The same pattern was followed by the other two super combos: Only Aaron ever hit more than 40 any other year and only Mantle had one other 50-plus season.

9

SERIES SLUGGERS

The Big Four

In the four Series in which Ruth and Gehrig played together (1926, '27, '28 and 1932), they were sensational. Check these figures for the 19 games: Each hit safely 27 times. They had 18 four-masters (Ruth 11, Gehrig 7). Ruth scored 25 runs, plated 22 and batted .409. Gehrig scored 17 times, knocked 25 across and averaged .422. Neither ever batted under .300 in these four showdowns.

Al Simmons and Jimmie Foxx pounded NL pitching with almost equal ferocity in the Athletics' three consecutive Series of 1929 through 1931. They teamed up to hit safely 45 times, clubbed half of all homers hit, scored 25 runs and drove 28 home. Their combined BA was .339. Neither of them batted less than .300 in any of the three Series either.

Look at these statistics for power personified by the four Hall of Famers:

		HR	Total	HR by Teammates	HR by Opponents	BA	GW	GL
1926	Ruth	4	4	0	4	.300	3	4
	Gehrig	0				.348		
1927	Ruth	2	2	0	0	.400	4	0
	Gehrig	0				.308		
1928	Ruth	3	7	2	1	.625	4	0
	Gehrig	4				.545		
1929	Simmons	2	4	2	1	.300	4	1
	Foxx	2				.350		
1930	Simmons	2	3	3	2	.364	4	2
	Foxx	1				.333		
1931	Simmons	2	3	0	2	.333	3	4
	Foxx	1				.348		
1931	Ruth	2	5	3	3	.333	4	0
1932	Gehrig	3				.529		
			28	10	13		26	11

Here is a summary of some of the other exploits of the four Big Hitters in the seven straight Series:

	"Big 4"	Rest of their team	
Runs	67	110	(38 percent)
RBI	75	92	(45 percent)
BA	.376	.219	

Ruth performed in six other Series (1915, '16 and '18 with the Red Sox and 1921–22–23 with the Yankees) and hit 15 homers overall. Gehrig appeared in three others (1936, '37 and '38) and drilled 10 home runs.

I know that superlatives are often over-worked, but ladies and gentlemen, boys and girls, I can only describe the numbers on the "Big Four" in those seven Series from 1926 through 1932 as CO-LOSSAL and STUPENDOUS!

The Mick and Yogi Show

The longest-running Series slugging show played over 13 years (1951–63). The leading home run performers were Mickey Mantle and Yogi Berra. They got their power act together 11 times for the Yankees (missing only 1954 and '59). In this span, they connected for most of the circuit blows

Three of the greatest Series sluggers, from left, LOU GEHRIG, JIMMIE FOXX, BABE RUTH.

which moved Mantle ahead of Ruth for the record number of homers in the October spectacle (18) and that propelled Berra past Gehrig into the number three career Series slot (12 and 10, respectively). (Duke Snider of the Dodgers, meanwhile, was moving into fourth place in all-time Series homers, also ahead of Gehrig.)

The power-actor duo of Mantle and Berra had some great performances, some average ones and a few that were downright embarrassing:

		HR	Total	HR by Teammates	HR by Opponents	BA	GW	GL
1951	Mantle	0	0	5	2	.200	4	2
	Berra	0				.261		
1952	Mantle	2	4	6	6	.345	4	3
	Berra	2				.214		
1953	Mantle	2	3	6	8	.208	4	2
	Berra	1				.429		
1955	Mantle	1	2	6	9	.200	3	4
	Berra	1				.417		
1956	Mantle	3	6	6	3	.250	4	3
	Berra	3				.360		
1957	Mantle	1	2	5	8	.263	3	4
	Berra	1				.320		
1958	Mantle	2	2	8	3	.250	4	3
	Berra	0				.272		
1960	Mantle	3	4	6	4	.400	3	4
	Berra	1				.318		
1961	Mantle	0	1	6	3	.167	4	1
	Berra	1				.273		
1962	Mantle	0	0	3	5	.120	4	3
	Berra	0				.000		
1963	Mantle	1	1	1	3	.133	0	4
	Berra	0				.000		
		25	58		54		37	33

Mantle played in one other Series ('64). His last was one of his best as he hit three homers, knocked in eight runs and batted .333. Berra was in three others (1947, '49 and '50). In his first Series he made the record books by getting the first pinch hit for the distance. He also knocked one out in '50.

Mickey and Yogi had a lot more help from their teammates than Babe and Lou or Al and Jimmie. And their team was not nearly as successful as the YankeeA's clubs of the 1926–32 period in terms of game-winning percentage, although the Yanks did win seven of the 11 Series they played in from '51 through '63.

Mr. October

No discussion of Series sluggers would be complete without mention of Reggie Jackson. Here is a summary of the performances which earned him the sobriquet "Mr. October":

Year	Team	HR	R	RBI	BA	GW	GL
1973	A's	1	3	6	.310	4	3
1974	A's	1	3	1	.286	4	1
1977	Yankees	5	10	8	.450	4	2
1978	Yankees	2	9	8	.438	4	2
1981	Yankees	1	3	1	.333	2	4
		10	28	24	.347	18	12

Would you believe that no AL team won the Series without Reggie on the roster for 12 straight years, 1971 through 1982? (Jackson was on the A's roster in 1972, but did not play.)

All Hail the Duke

Finally, Duke Snider of the Brooklyn-LA Dodgers also hammered out some impressive Series slugging statistics. In fact, if only his "prime time" Series years ('52–'53 and '55–'56) are included, the Silver Fox had 33 hits, 10 HR, 18 R, 24 RBI and a .327 BA, close to the accomplishments of Ruth, Gehrig and Jackson in their prime.

Year	HR	R	RBI	BA	GW	GL
1949	0	2	0	.143	1	4
1952	4	5	8	.345	3	4
1953	1	3	5	.320	2	4
1955	4	5	7	.320	4	3
1956	1	5	4	.304	3	4
1959	1	1	2	.200	4	2
	11	21	26	.286	17	21

To recap, the lifetime Series homer leaders are: Mantle 18, Ruth 15, Berra 12, Snider 11, Gehrig and Jackson, 10 each.

Series Quiz

Most of the home runs that made a difference in the outcome of a World Series, or that were record-setters or otherwise noteworthy are chronicled in the chapter, "Home Runs to Remember." The balance of this chapter is devoted to some important and not-so-important four-base hits spanning 79 Octobers. While not necessarily so important, the occurrences are all novel. The information on Series slugs and sluggers is provided in quiz form. Answers and spaces for scoring follow the quiz.

Points	Questions

Points **Questions**

3   1. What player hit two HR in three consecutive Series (six total)?

4   2. What player hit three HR in two consecutive Series (six total)?

4   3. Who was the only player to hit four HR in two different Series (8 total)? (a) Lou Gehrig (b) Duke Snider (c) Reggie Jackson

4   4. Which of these players did *not* hit two pinch-hit HR in one Series? (a) Dusty Rhodes (b) Chuck Essegian (c) Bernie Carbo

4   5. Who were the only brothers to hit HR in the same Series? (a) Paul and Lloyd Waner (b) Clete and Ken Boyer (c) Bob and Irish Meusel

6   6. The record for total HR in a Series (both teams) is 17. It was accomplished three times. The same two teams clashed all three times and each time the division was nine for one team, eight for the other. Who were the teams and what were the years? (Three points for the teams, one each for each correct year.)

5   7. The Yankees hit 10 or more HR in a single Series five times. What was the only other club to hit 10?

10   8. Nine players smacked two or more HR in a Series for their team's only HR (one did it twice). Who were they? (One point for each correct answer.)

6   9. Six players stroked two HR in a Series after hitting two or less in the regular season. Who were they? (One point for each correct answer.)

4   10. One player hit three HR in a Series after hitting only two for his team in the regular season. Who was he?

5
(bonus)   11. What player batted 1.000 in his only official Series at bat, and that only hit was a HR?

Points   **Answers**

1. Al Simmons (Philadelphia Athletics, 1929–30–31).
2. Goose Goslin (Washington Senators, 1924–25).
3. (b) Duke Snider (Brooklyn Dodgers, 1952 and '55).
4. (a) Dusty Rhodes
5. (b) Clete (New York Yankees) and Ken (St Louis Cardinals) Boyer in 1964. Ken cracked one in game four (a grand slam). Each delivered a bases-empty job in the final, seventh game, won by the Cardinals.
6.

TEAM HR

Year	Yankees	Dodgers
1953	9	8
1955	8	9
1977	8	9

7. The Baltimore Orioles (10 in 1970).

8.

Year	Player, Team	No. HR
1903	Patsy Dougherty, Boston Red Sox	2*
1909	Fred Clarke, Pittsburgh Pirates	2
1916	Larry Gardner, Boston Red Sox	2* +
1917	Benny Kauff, New York Giants	2*
1922	Aaron Ward, New York Yankees	2
1926	Babe Ruth, New York Yankees	4**
1927	Babe Ruth, New York Yankees	2+ +
1945	Hank Greenberg, Detroit Tigers	2
1954	Dusty Rhodes, New York Giants	2
1979	Willie Stargell, Pittsburgh Pirates	3

* — Both in one game
** — Three in one game
+ — Gardner also hit the Bosox' only HR in the 1912 classic.
+ + — Only two HR of series

Points   Answers

_____   9.

Year	Player, Team	HR in Series	HR in Season
1915	Harry Hooper, Boston Red Sox	2*	2
1916	Larry Gardner, Boston Red Sox	2*	2
1924	Bucky Harris, Washington Senators	2	1
1935	Frank Demaree, Chicago Cubs	2	2
1959	Chuck Essegian, LA Dodgers	2	1
1981	Willie Randolph, New York Yankees	2**	2

* — Both in one game
** — Also homered in AL championship series, for three HR in post-season play

_____   10. Ted Kluszewski (Chicago White Sox, 1959). "Klu" hit four HR total in the regular season; he parked two for the Pittsburgh Pirates before coming over to the Windy City team to finish the season.

_____   11. Jim Mason (New York Yankees, 1976).

Scoring: 45-55—Take your place at the head of the HR trivia class.
45-55—Take your place at the head of the HR trivia class.
35-44—You could probably write a book on home runs, too.
25-34—Above average fan.
Less than 25—Read the rest of this book and your score will improve!

Should CLIFF "CACTUS" CRAVATH be in the Hall of Fame? It's a prickly question.

George Brace Photo

10

CRUSHER CRAVATH

Clifford Carlton Cravath was popularly known as Gavvy and sometimes Cactus. Based on the following analysis, Crusher may have been a good nickname, too.

My story so far has been that, as far as the home run is concerned, in the beginning there was Babe Ruth. I've also said that 1920 was really the beginning of the Big Hitter era.

But what about those years 1901–1919 when a player could earn the name "Home Run" Baker by hitting 8 or 10 a year and a couple in the World Series and when whole *teams* might not hit 30?

It becomes necessary to construct a different formula to rank power hitters for 1901–19. Let's award one point for each career homer in the period, 10 for a league leadership (five for a tie), 10 more for reaching double digits and an additional five points for each five more homers in a year.

To illustrate the computations, let's take Babe Ruth's record in these years: He had 49 HR = 49 points; he tied for the league lead in 1918 (11) = 10 points and 1919 (29) = 25. Incidentally, he was the only performer in the period to hit more than 25 in a season and thus the only one to accumulate 25 points in this way.

Here are the ratings for those 19 years for all players with more than 75 "D-points."

| | | Points for: | | |
Player	HR in Period	League Leads	Double Digits	D-Points
1. Gavvy Cravath	118	55	90	263
2. Frank Baker*	80	35	50	165
3. Wildfire Schulte	92	15	50	157
4. Fred Luderus	84	0	50	134
5. Harry Davis	68	40	20	128
6. Sam Crawford*	89	20	15	124
7. Sherry Magee	83	0	40	123
8. Babe Ruth*	49	15	35	99
9. Larry Doyle	70	0	20	90
Vic Saier	55	0	35	90
11. Owen Wilson	59	0	30	89
12. Honus Wagner*	78	0	10	88
Buck Freeman**	48	10	30	88
14. Ty Cobb*	67	10	0	77
Heinie Zimmerman	57	10	10	77
16. Socks Seybold	51	10	15	76
Fred Merkle	56	0	20	76

* Hall of Fame
**Would have 157 points if pre-1901 homers included.

Other players with 60 or more D-points: Cy Williams 74, Tim Jordan 72, Nap Lajoie* 70, "Piano Legs" Hickman 69, Tommy Leach 66, Jimmy Sheckard 65, Wally Pipp 64, Tilly Walker 64, Dave Robertson 60, Tris Speaker* 60.

By these comparisons, Cravath is the runaway leader, almost 100 points better than Frank Baker. Is "Cactus" Cravath therefore Hall of Fame material? It's a prickly question.

11

HOME RUNS OF THE SECOND KIND . . .

We usually think of the home run as a towering fly ball or a rising line drive that leaves the confines of the playing field without anybody laying a glove on it. There is, of course, a second kind, one we don't see much anymore, that does not escape the field and remains in play: the inside-the-park home run.

The inside-the-park homer (IPH) may be a ground ball that eludes the fielders and then ricochets around long enough for the batter to circle the bases before a play can be made. Or, it could be a long triple daringly stretched into a four-base-hit by a lightning runner.

The IPH is decidedly a Big Hit because, like the wall-clearing variety, it always accomplishes the offensive team's ultimate objective; it scores a run. It is also dramatic and thrilling, just like the fence-clearing kind, maybe even more so because of the race around the bases and a possibility of a close play at the plate.

But, as one would expect, it ordinarily is not delivered by a big, powerful hitter, since speed is often the key ingredient. (However, Babe Ruth hit 10 IPH and Boog Powell, all 6-foot-5 and 240 pounds of him, authored one. It is not recorded that Frank Howard did.)

The Society for American Baseball Research (SABR) recently undertook a project to gather information about the within-bounds home run. In the 1980 *Baseball Research Journal*, Mil Chipp wrote that all of the questions haven't been answered about the IPH and that information is spotty and hard to come by, even for recent years. Chipp says, "The number and percentage of IPH have been gradually reduced since 1901, when about 35 percent were inside jobs."

The IPH is not unheard of these days, however. The *Journal* article calls to attention "the recent exploits of Willie Wilson of the Kansas City Royals. Of his six round-trippers in 1979, five were within bounds, a total that has not been achieved in many years." Kiki Cuyler's eight IPH (of 17 total Home Runs) in 1925 are credited as "the best season total in at least the last 60 years."

A minimum of three of the players declared Big Hitters of the 1901–1919 deadball era by "D-points" achieved a significant proportion of their totals via the IPH ramble. They were Sam Crawford, Ty Cobb and Tommy Leach. Crawford (D-6 in the rankings) had 97 career HR and 89 in the 1901–19 period. He is credited with having to leg out more than half of them, 51 total. Cobb (D-14) belted 118 four-masters in his career, including 68 in the deadball era. Of his 47 total IPH, 40 were collected before 1919. That means he had to race the throw more often than trot the base paths in the 1901-19 period, when IPH were more common. Leach (D-22), just 5'6½" and 150 pounds hit 62 homers in his playing days and had to scramble for 48 of them, according to SABR. Four were grand slams and "in 1903 he hit seven inside the park, including two in one game."

Other tidbits: Rabbit Maranville, the pint-sized Hall of Fame shortstop, hit 28 homers in 23 years and 22 were IPH. Tommy Thevenow hit two homers in 1,229 games, both through inside work. He collected another in the 1926 World Series (it got by Ruth). At the other end of the spectrum, Ted Williams counted one among his 521 homers as an IPH. Yep, it was accomplished against the Williams (or Boudreau) shift. Toby Harrah and Bump Wills circled the bases on hits off two consecutive pitches while the ball was still in play for the Rangers in a game at Yankee Stadium in 1977.

The SABR article concludes that "IPH's are essentially an extension of the three-base hit." That would seem logical for Cuyler's 1925 performance. He scurried to a league-leading 26 three-baggers that year, good for a three-way tie for second on the all-time triples-in-a-season list. Sam Crawford (1914) and Joe Jackson (1912) were the others who hit 26 triples in a year. Only Owen (Chief) Wilson hit more (36 in 1911). Incidentally, Wilson set the record on the last day of the season and was out at home trying to stretch the triple into an IPH.

Based on the "triple hitters are also IPH hitters" finding, the following pre-Ruthian BH besides Crawford, Cobb and Leach who compiled a big bunch of D points with IPH are: Sherry Magee (D-7), Larry Doyle (D-9T), Owen Wilson (D11), Honus Wagner (D-12) and Nap Lajoie (D-20).

I couldn't tell you who hit the first IPH. But I do know who authored the first IBH (Inside-the-Building Homer). The enclosed Houston Astrodome opened with an exhibition game on April 9, 1965. U.S. President Lyndon Johnson was there. Texas Governor John Connally threw out the first ball. Mickey Mantle was there, too, and hit the first indoors HR. But the Astros edged the Yankees 2-1.

12

. . . AND THE THIRD DIMENSION

I propose a third class of home run: the One that Got Away (OGA). Numerous homers are washed away with incomplete games. Some are snatched away when an outfielder reaches over and/or above the wall to haul in a drive headed for the seats ("He was robbed!").

Lou Gehrig got an OGA in a most unusual way. In a regular-season game in 1931, he parked one in the center field stands in Washington's Griffith Stadium. But, football-like, the ball bounced back into play and a Senator outfielder clapped on to it. The runner ahead of the Iron Horse, Lyn Lary, saw only the catch as he rounded second. Assuming the third out, he jogged past the bag at third and headed for the dugout, unnoticed by Joe McCarthy in the third base coaching box. Gehrig, also unaware that Lary had left the field ahead of him, continued toward home and was called out for passing a runner.

Hank Aaron once deposited a Curt Simmons delivery atop the roof in St. Louis' Sportsman's Park for an apparent HR. But the ump ruled Aaron out instead because he was not in the batter's box when he connected. Hank had thus found another way to collect an OGA.

Lost his cap but caught the ball. AL GIONFRIDDO'S great snag of JOE DIMAGGIO'S long drive in the '47 Series.

One of the most celebrated OGA robberies was Al Gionfriddo's catch of Joe DiMaggio's 415-foot drive with two Yankee runners on base in the 1947 World Series. An otherwise obscure part-time outfielder, Gionfriddo's heroic grab helped save that sixth game victory for the Brooks, but the next day the Yankees did the Dodgers in again.

Perhaps the most controversial OGA got away from the Pirates' Earl Smith in the 1925 World Series. To set the scene: The score is 4–3 in favor of the Senators in the eighth inning of game three. Smith catches up to a Firpo Marberry pitch and powers it to the far reaches of Griffith Stadium. It appears to be headed for the bleachers. Center fielder Sam Rice races back, leaps and appears to catch the ball. But he tumbles over the railing and disappears. The crowd, the players and the umpires strain to see what happened. In due time, Rice reappears, holding the ball. Whether Sam actually hung on or dropped it as he went over constitutes the controversy (the score stands up and the Nats defeat the Bucs). Regardless, it was ruled a catch by the umpire, so an out it was and, clearly, it was One that Got Away.

There are also the long, loud foul ("if he had only straightened that one out . . . "), the drive to a deep part of playing territory which is caught (" . . . would have gone out in such-and-such park") and the one that " . . . just missed a HR by inches." Examples are Mays' back-to-the-plate snare of Vic Wertz's 440-foot fly in the '54 Series and Joe Rudi's game-saving catch against the left field fence in the '72 Series.

These are not OGA, however. They're IF Onlies (IFO). In that same Series in which Rice robbed Smith of a bleacher blast, there was also a clear case of an IFO. The scene shifts to Pittsburgh's Forbes Field. It is the ninth inning of game six with the Pirates leading 3–2. The Nats' Joe Harris, who has already clubbed three Series HR, takes one to deep CF. The ball would have been out of the park during the regular season, but a temporary screen had been erected for the Series. Harris' drive hits high off the barrier and remains in play. He gets a double instead of a home run and dies on base. The Pirates whip the Senators in the game by one run and go on to win the Series by one game. It's an IFO, because "IF Only the screen hadn't been there . . . " But it was, and baseball is not horseshoes. Close doesn't count. So there's no way an IFO can be classed in the same category as an OGA.

There are some interesting IFO's regarding Babe Ruth and Jimmie Foxx. IF Only there had been a screen in front of the right field pavilion in Sportsman's Park, St. Louis, Ruth might have hit fewer than 60 HR in 1927. He hit four in that park but it is unrecorded if any of them dropped into the open pavilion rather than going over its roof. A screen was erected in 1929. So, conversely, IF Only there had NOT been a screen in front of the pavilion seats in 1932, Foxx would have hit more than his season's total of 58. (It is known that Foxx hit several drives against the screen.)

Perhaps still another kind of HR should be added to the IPH, OGA and IFO lexicon: the IGH (It's a Gift Homer). This type includes balls that rolled or bounced under, through or over fences—or into the crowd where there were no fences—in the days before ground rule doubles. Other examples are Cesar Cedeno's 200-foot grand slam courtesy of colliding fielders (see "Short Takes" chapter) and Rocky Nelson's game-winning IPH-IGH in a 1949 game between the Cubs and the Cardinals. Cub outfielder Andy Pafko thought he caught Nelson's drive to end the game with the Chicagoans leading 3–2. But umpire Al Barlick ruled a trap and Nelson circled the basepaths behind another runner for a 4–3 St. Louis win while Pafko ran in with the ball in his hand.

There's no one that I know of who has tried to total up what batters had the most career OGA or what fielders executed the most Homer Take Aways (HTA). But maybe I'd better keep this on the QT. In this figure-mad, computer-infested, acronym-happy world, somebody's Likely to Try It (LTI).

HANK GREENBERG *hit the Grandest Slam.*

13

THE GRANDEST SLAMS

Grand slam: It's the most descriptive term possible for the, well, grandest kind of home run, the one hit with the bases loaded. Yet, this special kind of four-bagger almost defies description.

Let's take the words one by one and then put them together. "Grand" is variously described in dictionaries as "having more importance than others," "notably large and great," "fine or imposing in impression," "illustrious, eminent or foremost." The words that spring from it suggest all these things and more: grandeur, grandiloquence, grandiose, grande dame and, yes, even grand larceny and the Grand Canyon. One dictionary sets it apart by saying: "Grand is distinguished from other words meaning huge or colossal by its implications of handsomeness and dignity."

Now the word "slam" is something else again. It's easy to find words to describe it: "A heavy blow," "a noisy closing" or "a violent criticism." It doesn't spin off other words. It's just its loud, violent self.

Thus, "grand slam" becomes a study in contrasts. It's the penthouse and the furnace room, eloquent French and guttural German, an imposing impact, a handsome blow, a notably great criticism (of the opposing pitcher, perhaps?).

The grand slam, therefore, is just about beyond description and sometimes almost beyond belief.

There have been two grand slams hit in the same inning, two hit by the same batter in two consecutive innings. One was hit by a 41-year-old man (Honus Wagner).

A pitcher (Tony Cloninger) was the first and only player in the National League to hit two grand slams in one game.

Pinch hitters on opposing teams (Pat Crawford of the Giants and Les Bell of the Braves) each socked a slam in one game.

Indicative of the rarity of the grand slam is that it took five years of organized ball before anybody could hit one (Roger Connor in 1881), until 1920 before any mortal (Elmer Smith) could unload one in a World Series, until 1966 when Cloninger performed his feat and a half century before anyone (Fred Lynn) got an All-Star game slammer.

I think it's fairly easy to pick out the single grandest slam. Here's the scene: It's the last day of the season in 1945. The Tigers are to play the Browns in St. Louis. If the Bengals can win this, the 153rd game of the season, they can clinch the pennant. If not, they'll have to play no. 154, because they're only a game ahead of the Senators, who have already finished up. But it's raining, just as it has been for days. The rain finally stops and the game begins. The defending Champion Brownies, although out of it this year, prove to be real gamers. They battle from behind and lead the Tigers 3–2 in the ninth, with the skies darkening and threatening rain again. The Tigers load the bases with one out for Hank Greenberg. The count goes to 1 and 1 and then, you know the rest, the big man sends the next pitch into the left field bleachers for game, pennant and season.

That may have been the most dramatic and decisive four-run home run ever hit, but every one of them is, how can I say it any better: a GRAND SLAM.

HITTING IN A PINCH

Jerry Lynch is the all-time leader in pinch-hit homers with 18. He has only one challenger to the title, Cliff Johnson, who is tied with three other players with 16 career pinch-hit home runs. Every other player who has hit 10 or more HR as a substitute batter has finished his career.

The leaders through 1982:
Jerry Lynch—18
Gates Brown, Smoky Burgess, Cliff Johnson, Willie McCovey—16
George Crowe—14
Joe Adcock, Bob Cerv—12
Fred Whitfield, Cy Williams—11
Don Mincher, Wally Post, Gus Zernial—10

How hard is it to come in off the bench, often in a tight situation, and do a good job?

The pressure of hitting in a pinch got to Lynch as far as getting a hit, but not in going for the downs. Jerry averaged .260 pinch-hitting, .280 as a full-time player. But his proportion of home runs to at bats was the same, 4.0 percent, whether he was coming off the bench cold or coming in from the

JERRY LYNCH is the all-time leader in pinch-hit homers.

George Brace Photo

field to hit. Another of the leaders, Burgess, likewise had a little lower BA as a pinch-hitter than as a regular lineup entry (.288 to .296). He responded to being on the spot as a pinch-hitter more favorably for hitting the long ball, however. His pinch-hitting percentage of HR was 3.2, compared to 2.8 when he was catching and hitting.

Some pinch-hitting achievements not otherwise noted in other sections of this book:

The Reds' Art Shamsky did about all that is humanly possible to try to win one against the Pirates in a 1966 game, but to no avail. Called in to pinch-hit in the eighth inning, he drubbed a HR. But the game was tied at the end of regulation and went into extra innings. Shamsky stayed in the lineup and did his best to win it for the Reds in the 10th and again in the 11th, as he homered two more times. But the Pirates won.

On two different occasions, Chicago Cub playing managers had bases-loaded game situations and figured the strategy called for a pinch-hitter. Each time, they looked over their bench, shook their heads and picked out a bat for themselves. Each time they delivered pinch-hit grand slammers. The playing manager-strategists were Rogers Hornsby in 1931 and Phil Cavarretta, who duplicated Hornsby's feat 20 years later in 1951.

15

PITCHERS AS HITTERS AND VICE VERSA

Pitchers as Hitters

Wes Ferrell was one of the game's best pitchers. He won 20 or more games in his first four complete seasons and eventually had six 20-W campaigns. Unlike most moundsmen, he was also dangerous with a bat in his hands. He had a .280 lifetime BA, socked 38 HR, the record for pitchers, and was frequently called on to pinch-hit, although he hit a pinch-hit home run only once. Five times he knocked two out in one game, another record for pitchers. His brother Rick, a catcher, batted .281 lifetime and managed only 28 homers, even though he had 1,884 career AB to Wes' 548.

Of course, Wes did not always share in the backslapping and general glee that follows a home run. He gave up a few pitching. In 1937, for instance, he was on the unhappy end of 25 round-trippers hit off his pitching by enemy batsmen. That performance landed him in a tie that year for most HR allowed by a pitcher in the AL.

The brothers Ferrell had their careers intertwine in unusual ways on two occasions. In 1931, Wes worked a no-hitter for the Indians. One of the opposing batsmen to whom he showed no mercy was brother Rick, Browns catcher. Wes hit a home run and a double, driving in four runs in the

If there are American League Pitchers today who can hit 'em out like WES
FERRELL used to, we'll never know, because of the designated hitter.
George Brace Photo

7–0 gem. Two years later, Wes and Rick both hit HR in a game Wes was
pitching for the Tribe and Rick was catching for the Red Sox. It was the only
time both homered in the same game, even though they played in the AL at
the same time for 11 years.

If there are American League pitchers today who can hit 'em out like Wes Ferrell used to, we'll never know. The designated hitter has snatched the bat away from them. At this writing, it has been more than 10 years since an American League pitcher has hit a home run in a regular-season game (Roric Harrison of the Orioles in 1972).

Wes Ferrell wasn't the only pitcher who had sensational pitching-power days. Rick Wise spiced up his no-hitter by rapping two HR as the Phils whipped the Reds 4–0. Red Ruffing cracked a 10th-inning swat to reward himself with a 1–0 win. Jim Tobin lofted three consecutive HR as he also pitched and won a game, 6–5 for the Braves. Ken Brett hit homers in four straight games in which he pitched. Tony Cloninger hit two grand slams in one game.

In a 1953 game, third baseman Vern Stephens was scheduled to come to bat with the bases jammed in the ninth. He had 10 career grand slams, so what better could a manager ask for? White Sox manager Paul Richards knew what to ask for: the second guess of the century as he waved in pitcher Tommy Byrne to pinch-hit. Byrne, facing one of the most fearsome fireballers of all time, Ewell Blackwell, smacked a grand slam off the Yankee hurler.

Long, long ago, in 1906, another crafty manager, Connie Mack, short on players in the sixth inning, called on star pitcher Chief Bender to patrol the outfield for the Athletics in a game against the Red Sox. Bender zapped two homers, both inside-the-park productions, and the Mackmen won the game.

Hitters as Pitchers

The Red Sox were being chewed up by the Tigers in a 1940 game. Big Hitter Ted Williams (No.14 in the N-ratings), was called to the mound to finish up. Regular Red Sox hurlers had been rattled for 11 runs by the Detroit team, including a homer, double, two singles and five RBI by Rudy York. Terrible Ted allowed only three hits and one run in two innings. He succeeded where other Boston pitchers had failed with York: Ted struck him out on three pitches. But the Tigers won 12–1.

Twenty-eight years later, almost to the day, BH Rocky Colavito (N-20) was summoned to pitch in an emergency situation on behalf of the Yankees. Colavito's former team, the Tigers, were again the antagonists. Rocky surrendered but one hit in 2$\frac{2}{3}$ innings and picked up the win when the Big Apple team rallied to win 6–5. In the second game, the Rock returned to his more natural position as an outfielder and hit a homer as the Yanks swept the twin bill with a 5–4 win.

Vice Versa

As a pitcher, Babe Ruth was a good hitter. As a hitter, he was a good pitcher. Ruth the pitcher had one of the great winning percentage records ever (better than 67 percent), twice won 20 or more games and had a 3–0 record and 29²/₃ consecutive shutout innings in Series competition. Even after the Yankees got him and made him a full-time outfielder, the Babe appeared as a pitcher in five games (1920, 1921, 1930 and 1933) and won them all! He pitched a complete game victory at age 38.

During the transition years of 1918–19 with the Red Sox, as he started dividing his time between pitching and the outfield, he had some fine pitching-power numbers. In 1918, Ruth had 13 W and 11 HR (tied for league lead); in 1919, pitching still less and hitting still more, he had 9 W and 29 HR (league lead). That's 22 W and 40 HR or a combined W-HR total of 62.

Another possibly promising pitching career by a Big Hitter was nipped in the bud because of the end of World War II. Here's how that came about:

Jimmie Foxx (N-7), after being released by Portsmouth of the Piedmont League following the 1944 season, caught on with the Phillies for the last war year, 1945. The Beast played in 54 games at first and third, batting .268 and cracking seven homers. But so thin was the talent in organized ball and particularly in Philadelphia (the Phils finished eighth at 46–108), that Foxx was asked to take to the hill in nine games. War or no war, the 37-year old acquitted himself admirably. He started two games, had a 1–0 record and a Foxxy 1.59 ERA. He mowed down opposing batters on strikes 10 times in 23 innings pitched, while permitting 13 hits and walking 14.

But when the boys came marching home in 1946, there was no spot for Jimmie on anybody's roster.

Foxx had previously pitched only one big league inning as a stunt for the Red Sox in 1939. The '39 appearance was what the Boston *Globe* called "(manager) Joe Cronin's annual insult to his regular mound corps." The *Globe* also rated the 1940 appearance of Williams on the mound in the same "insult" category.

Foxx, incidentally, narrowly missed catching Williams in the 1940 contest. He started the game behind the plate but retired to rest for the second game of that day's double header. Thus, quoting from an article by Tom Hufford in the 1978 *Baseball Research Journal*, "it ruined a chance for baseball's 'greatest home run battery'." That same article notes that "Joe Glenn was behind the plate for Williams, and he was the same journeyman backstop who caught the last game pitched by Babe Ruth in 1933."

***PHIL NIEKRO** has knuckled up a few gopher balls in his career.*
Courtesy Atlanta Braves

16

GO-PHER IT

While we're taking this time to heap credit on the batters who excel in hitting home runs, let's pause to dump some discredit on the pitchers who allow them to be hit.

Robin Roberts is the most notorious gopher ball pitcher of all time. It was a rare game when Robin wasn't rocked for a home run. He watched 502 of his pitches sail off into the blue in his career, the only pitcher to surrender more than 500. However, Ferguson Jenkins just might wrest the title from Roberts before he's through. Fergie had been flogged for 465 four-baggers through 1982.

Besides his career record in home runs allowed (HRA), Robin gave up more in one season than anybody ever has (46 in 1956), led the league in gopher balls four years in a row (1954–57) and also tied for the most in 1960. He was the first to surrender 300 and 400 as well as the only one to date to attain 500 HRA.

Jenkins stood and watched some of his grooved pitches go out of sight as many or more times as any other pitcher in seven different campaigns, five times (including one tie) with the Cubs in the National League and twice with the Rangers in the American.

Roberts was one of the great modern-day control pitchers in addition to being the gopher ball champion. When he set the single-season record for total HRA in 1956, he walked only 40. Jenkins also has a history of being generous with home runs but stingy with free passes. In '71, he allowed more home runs than anybody in the league, but walked only 37 batters and posted a sterling won-loss record. Here are the records for Robin's and Fergie's league-leading HRA years:

Player, Team	Year	HRA	IP/HR	BB	W-L
Roberts, Phils	1954	35	9.6	56	23–15
	1955	41	7.4	5 3	23–14
	1956	46	6.5	40	19–18
	1957	40	6.25	43	10–22
	1960	31 (tie)	7.6	34	12–16
		193	7.4	226	87–85
Jenkins, Cubs	1967	30	9.6	83	20–13
	1968	26 (tie)	11.8	65	20–15
	1971	29	11.2	37	24–13
	1972	32	9.0	62	20–12
	1973	35	7.7	57	14–16
Rangers	1975	37	7.3	56	17–18
	1979	40	6.5	81	16–14
		229	8.8	441	131–101

It's hard to argue with the success of twirlers like Roberts and Jenkins, high HRA or no.

Some other high career HRA have been suffered by Warren Spahn (434), Jim Kaat (390), Gaylord Perry (375), Phil Niekro and Catfish Hunter (374 each) and Jim Bunning (372), all reasonably good at getting the ball over the plate. If there's a pattern here (and following discussion will dispute that there is), it's that control pitchers are the most frequent HRA victims.

In theory, the message the control pitcher sends to the batter is: "Here comes a pitch in the strike zone. See if you can hit it."

The batter responds, in effect: "I know you're not wild. I can't stand around here waiting for bad pitches and a possible free ticket to first base. I'll dig in and take a good cut."

The pitching-batting psych thus sometimes results in long hits. But, by forcing the swing, an out may result instead. Also, the control pitcher will tend to give up solo shots, rather than two-and three-run homers which can evolve from walking preceding batters. Jim Palmer, a pretty good control pitcher, has never been reached for a grand slam homer through almost 4,000 innings of pitching.

On the flip side, wild fireballers may be the toughest to solve for home runs.

For example, the best batting strategy against Nolan Ryan of the Angels in 1977 was to keep the body loose and the bat still. If he got it over, you couldn't hit it. He struck out 341 and allowed only 12 home runs in 299 innings, both tops in the AL. But if a batter stayed loose in order to jump out of the way of the wild, inside pitches and took all the rest, he might get on base. Ryan walked 204 batters, also tops in the majors and second all-time (Bob Feller issued 208 BB in 1938).

Nolan is one of the flamethrowers who has had a good record in recent years in HRA. Through 1982, he had surrendered 181 HR in 3,325 innings pitched (1 HRA/18.4 IP). Other hard throwers who did well, according to researcher Raymond Gonzalez, were Bob Veale, 91 HRA/1,926 IP $= \frac{1}{21.2}$ and J.R. Richard before his illness, 73 HRA/1,606 IP $= \frac{1}{22}$.

But these HRA records are exceedingly pale when stacked up against the pitchers of yesteryear. Prior to 1920, before the Big Hitter Era began, the pitchers with the lowest HRA records usually gave up zero.

Walter Johnson had the most remarkable year in avoiding the gopher pitch. In 1916, he surrendered none in 371 innings. That same year, another AL pitcher was second to Johnson and recorded the fourth-best record in history for dodging the home run. It was none other than Babe Ruth, Red Sox pitcher, who had 0 HRA in 324 IP.

One Ed Killian of the Tigers comes in third and sixth in season performances for working a lot of innings without being roughed up by long ball hitters. In 1904, Killian avoided the long hit in 332 innings; the next year, he escaped bomb threats in 313. But that's only part of the story. Killian, in a kind of Arabian nights fantasy, went 1,001 innings without surrendering a homer over almost a four-year period—from September 19, 1903, to August 7, 1907, according to Gonzalez.

Gonzalez has determined that, among pitchers with significant innings pitched, Big Ed Walsh was the most difficult homer-allower in history (24 HR/2,964 IP = one every 123.5 innings). The easiest touch was Pedro Ramos. In 2,355 innings, opposing batters feasted off his pitching to the tune of one home run every 7.5 innings.

The HRA statistics confirm that the Big Hitter Era began in 1920. Before that year, "0 for X" HRA ratios were common. Beginning in 1920, only one pitcher who has worked more than 154 innings (162 after 1961) has not been victimized for at least one around-the-horn hit. Al Sothoron turned the trick in 1921 (0 HRA/178 IP) while playing with the Browns, Red Sox and Indians. Possibly by staying on the move from one club to the next, Sothoron avoided facing Ruth that year, for by this time, the Babe was terrorizing pitchers rather than intimidating batters as he had in 1916. That year, 1921, Ruth smote the new record of 59 HR.

The last pitcher to work more than 154 innings and give up only one home run was Ewell Blackwell in 1946 (1 HRA/194 IP).

To dramatize how the long hit changed the game beginning in 1920, consider this: When Tommy John permitted 13 HR in 1980, with the Yankees, that was the *fewest* HR allowed in the AL for a pitcher with more than 162 IP. In 1919, Wilbur Cooper of the Pirates was reached for 10 HR. That was the *most* HRA in the NL by any pitcher for the season. Cooper allowed one circuit clout every 28.7 innings, John one every 20.4. Other similar performances could be cited for the two eras.

Earlier in this chapter there was a parenthetical statement that a later discussion would dispute that careful pitchers give up more home runs than wild chuckers.

The disputing evidence includes:

Phil Niekro of the Braves simultaneously allowed the most HR and the most bases on balls in the National League in 1979. Forty-one times he knuckled up pitches which batters proceeded to pole-ax. He walked 113. Maybe knuckle ballers are special cases. But other pitchers have had poor HRA years coupled with poor BB ratios and some have allowed relatively few HR while also walking relatively few.

Also, good HRA/IP and lousy HRA/IP have resided in some pitching arms in different years. A recent example of this type applies to A's pitcher Matt Keough. In 1978, he permitted the fewest HR among regular starters, 9 in 197 IP or 1 HR/22 IP. Four years later, his name showed up on the other side of the ledger. In 1982, Keough was blasted for 38 HR in 200 IP, one HRA every 5.5 innings. Others who have tasted the bitter and the sweet on different occasions include Bob Gibson, Lew Burdette and—are you ready for this—Walter Johnson. Yep, the same Walter Johnson who skunked the sluggers for 371 innings in 1916 was the same one who was reached for nine HR in 1913, more than any other AL hurler.

The imperfect conclusion reached is that a lot of factors, like velocity, control and innings pitched in a season and career, apparently all contribute to HRA statistics.

To return to the opening sentence of this chapter, it could also be that we should give the credit to the batters who can nail those pitches rather than lingering over the characteristics of those who serve 'em up. Finally, there are no doubt elements of luck—a pitching inch here and a swinging inch there can make a whale of a difference. And after all, as it's so often recited, baseball is a game of inches.

17

THE BIG WHIFFERS

If the Big Hitter fails to get the Big Hit, he often gets the Big Miss instead. He strikes out. Yes, Big Hitters are also Big Whiffers.

Mickey Mantle, for instance, fanned more than three times for every homer he hit (1,710 SO, 536 HR). In Mick's defense, however, I must note that he got on base by not swinging the bat more often than he flailed and failed; he drew 1,734 walks.

Before about 1950, striking out more than 100 times was sufficient to gain notoriety. Vince DiMaggio's 134 "K's" in 1938 was the record for batter frustration for 18 years. Today, a player has to be out on strikes in the neighborhood of 150 times before the catcalls start. Indeed, there have been five instances of players whiffing 175 times or more—more than once a game! — since the early '60s.

Jimmie Foxx led the AL in striking out seven times and Vince DiMaggio took the dishonor six times. Babe Ruth and Hack Wilson achieved the dubious distinction five times each. Their modern challengers are Reggie Jackson, five leaderships and Mantle, five (including two ties).

Jackson has the most career K's. His league-leading 156 whiffs in 1982 enabled him to take the "honor" away from Willie Stargell, who closed out his career in '82 with 1,936 total strikeouts. Reggie's record, meanwhile, soared to 1,966. The other top career cut-and-miss men are Bobby Bonds (1,757), Tony Perez (1,742), Lou Brock (1,730) and Mickey Mantle.

As for "big years," Bonds' '69–'70 performance is unchallenged for futility. He was thumbed on strikes 187 times in '69, shattering Dave Nicholson's '63 mark of 175. The next year was just as ignominious for Bobby. He fanned 189 times. Only Mike Schmidt and Gorman Thomas have come close since.

So who is the biggest Whiffer of them all? Foxx? Jackson? Bonds? Somebody else? Just as in home runs, I combine three categories (career, league leads and big-number seasons) to come up with the answer. A comparison of Big Whiffers follows.

I award (or, if you wish, penalize) the perpetrator with (1) 1 point per 10 career strikeouts, (2) 10 points for a league lead and (3) the following schedule for big-whiff seasons: Before 1950: 10 points for 100 SO, 10 additional for 125 or more; 1950 and after: 10 points for 125 SO, 10 more for 150, another 10 for 175 and up.

Here's how that figures out for the top 20 in "K-Points" through 1982:

Player	(Rank)*	Career SO No.	= Points	League Leads	Big–Season "Bonus"	K-Points
1. *Reggie Jackson*	(1)	1966	196	50	120	366
2. Bobby Bonds	(3)	1757	175	30	130	335
3. Richie Allen	(9)	1556	155	20	60	255
4. *Willie Stargell*	(2)	1936	193	10	50	253
5. *Dave Kingman*	(18)	1400	140	30	80	250
6. Mickey Mantle	(6)	1710	171	40	20	231
7. *Mike Schmidt*		1279	127	30	70	227
8. Jimmie Foxx		1311	131	70	20	221
9. *Lee May*	(8)	1570	157	10	40	207
10. Vince DiMaggio		837	83	60	60	203
11. Harmon Killebrew	(7)	1699	169	10	20	199
12. Frank Howard	(14)	1460	146	10	40	196
13. *Tony Perez*	(4)	1742	174	0	20	194
14. Lou Brock	(5)	1730	173	0	20	193
15. Jimmy Wynn	(16)	1427	142	10	40	192
16. *Greg Luzinski*		1298	129	10	50	189
17. *Gorman Thomas*		933	93	25	70	188
18. Donn Clendenon		1140	114	20	50	184
19. Babe Ruth		1330	133	50	0	183
20. George Scott	(17)	1418	141	10	30	181

*Rank among top 20 swingers; other top career SO victims not listed: Willie McCovey (10), Frank Robinson (11), Willie Mays (12), Eddie Mathews (13), Rick Monday (15), Hank Aaron (19) and Carl Yastrzemski (20).

DICK ALLEN, one of the Big Whiffers.

Courtesy Chicago White Sox

These data show Jackson to be the Whiff King (or should I call him Misschief?). Bonds and Richie Allen are 2–3. Kingman and Schmidt could challenge Jackson if they keep on cuttin'! Apparently the credo of Reggie, Bobby and Mike and other Big Whiffers is: "'Tis better to have swung and swished than never to have swung at all."

Of the 54 Big Hitters listed earlier, 14 are among the top 20 Big Whiffers and 16 are among the top 20 in career SO.

Other interesting observations:

1.   One of the first impressions: What is the name of little Lou Brock doing among all these big lumbermen? The 170-pound all-time base stealer averaged less than eight HR a year over 19 seasons and has no Big Hitter credentials, although he did hit one into the center field bleachers in the Polo Grounds as a Cub against the Mets in 1962. (The other possible exceptions are Vince DiMaggio, who averaged just 12.5 four-baggers a year over 10 summers and Clendenon who averaged 13 a year in 12 years.) Maybe Lou's abandon on the base paths carried over to the batter's box. Then, too, runner-up Bonds was an accomplished base stealer as well as a power hitter. Thus, another theory: A flock of strikeouts can be tolerated if your man can make up for his third strike sins with the big blast or the burgled bag.

2.   Ruth never struck out 100 times in a season in his career; 93 was his high. Jackson has averaged 123 SO a year.

3.   Much ink flows in favor of pitchers who record a large number of strikeouts, fellows like Walter Johnson, Bob Feller, Sandy Koufax, Bob Gibson and Nolan Ryan, to name a handful. While the victors of the pitch-and-miss war are venerated, precious little is written about the victims, chaps like Boots Grantham of the Cubs and Bobby Darwin of the Twins. After all, they got some bold ink in their records, too. Grantham led the NL in swinging and missing two years in a row, 1923–24 and Darwin paced the AL three times in succession, 1972–74. It's the American Way to accentuate the positive and eliminate the negative. If you don't believe that, try this trivia: Name any of the St. Louis Browns who led the league in striking out from 1913 (the first year such AL records were kept) through 1953 (the Browns' last year). *Answer:* Gus Williams (120 in 1914—a major league record that endured for 24 years), Doc Lavan (83 in '15), Marty McManus (69 in '25), Bruce Campbell (104 in '32), Harlond Clift (100 in '34), Chet Laabs (105 in '43), and Dick Kokos (91 in '49). You remember the stellar performances of all those diamond stars, don't you? Sure you do.

4.   The heyday of the K came in the '60s. Major league teams were averaging well over 900 strikeouts per club per year. In the early '50s, teams had averaged in the 600s and in the '20s and '30s in the 500s or less. The 971 K average per team in 1967 was the all-time high. The lowering of the mound and the shrinking of the strike zone in 1969 has had some effect; the average has receded. From 1978 through 1980, the average was back down below 800 per club per year. No wonder the "strikeout artists" of today are passing the mound masters of earlier years. Makes you wonder how Walter Johnson's hummer compared with Don Drysdale's. Or, if Ruth

and Foxx were better or worse calculators at the plate than Jackson and Killebrew. In other words, it's one of those indeterminate puzzles. Do we have greater strikeout pitchers in the modern game than in past decades or are there just more butchers at the bat, swinging more and connecting less?

5. Plain old batting ineptitude often took the batter strikeout title in the past. Barney Friberg fanned 77 times for the 1926 Phillies to lead all National League comers; he had one home run. Nick Cullop had 86 Ks to lead the NL for the Reds in 1931; he had eight homers. It was also his last year in the big leagues.

A distinguished few have achieved the glorious and the inglorious all at once—leading the league in HR and SO in the same season:

AMERICAN LEAGUE				NATIONAL LEAGUE			
Year	Player	HR	SO	Year	Player	HR	SO
1916	Wally Pipp	12	82	1927	Hack Wilson	30x	70
1918	Babe Ruth	11x	58	1928	Hack Wilson	31x	94
1923	Babe Ruth	41	89	1930	Hack Wilson	56	84
1924	Babe Ruth	46	81	1946	Ralph Kiner	23	109
1927	Babe Ruth	60	89	1971	*Willie Stargell*	48	154
1928	Babe Ruth	54	87	1974	*Mike Schmidt*	36	138
1933	Jimmie Foxx	48	93	1975	*Mike Schmidt*	38	180
1935	Jimmie Foxx	36x	99	1976	*Mike Schmidt*	38	149
1951	Gus Zernial	33	101	1979	*Dave Kingman*	48	131
1952	Larry Doby	32	111x	1982	*Dave Kingman*	37	156
1958	Mickey Mantle	42	120x				
1960	Mickey Mantle	40	125				
1962	Harmon Killebrew	48	142				
1979	*Gorman Thomas*	45	175				
1981	*Tony Armas*	22xx	115				
1982	*Reggie Jackson*	39x	156				

x — 2-way tie
xx — 4-way tie

ACTIVE PLAYERS IN 1982 IN ITALIC

One player and one player only gathered up a "double glorious" award. Tommy Holmes led the National League in home runs in 1945 with 28. He was also the toughest man to strike out. He fanned only nine times in 636 official plate appearances.

18

LIFE BEGINS AT 40

The saying "Life begins at 40" doesn't usually apply to baseball players. But for some, reaching the age of 40 doesn't necessarily mean the end of a career on the diamond. A select few play to that age and beyond. And some of them continue to hit with power.

Cy Williams tied for the league leadership in home runs the year he turned 40.

Six players managed 10 or more four-baggers the years they celebrated their 41st birthdays.

Ted Williams cracked 29 the year he attained age 42. The Thumper went out in style, whopping a big blow in his last major league at bat.

Carl Yastrzemski slammed 16 balls into the seats the year he reached age 43.

Ted Williams accomplished a feat you may never see in the record books, but one which will delight all those who admire the durability of the Carl Yastrzemski-George Blanda-Gordie Howe-Sam Snead-type athletes of our times. The Splendid Splinter thumped 65 homers as a 40-and-over performer, making him the record holder.

Yaz began the '83 season with a great chance to set the standard for 44 year-olds and the over-40 mark as well. At the end of the '82 season, he was just six behind Williams and ranked third on the all-time 40-plus list. Some of the other plus-40s may have added more to their totals had they had the designated hitter advantage accorded Yaz.

Two other geriatric achievements deserve mention. Although I have not included pre-1901 player performances in this book, Cap Anson's over-40 exploits deserve recognition. Born in 1851, Cub Cap played regularly through 1897, when he was 46. In those last seven, 40 and up years, he drummed 21 homers. Cap capped his 27-year career by cracking two homers on his final playing day. He was the oldest player ever to homer in the majors. Luke Appling, whose name does appear in the following list, hit a home run in an old-timers game in 1982. He was 75.

The players who have hit 10 or more home runs in their 40's:

| Player (Birth Date) | HOME RUNS IN YEAR REACHED AGE: | | | | TOTAL |
	40	41	42	43	
1. Ted Williams 8/30/18	26	10	29	DNP	65
2. Stan Musial 11/21/20	17	15	19	12	63
3. Carl Yastrzemski 8/22/39	21	15	7	16	59
4. Cy Williams 12/21/87	30xx	12	5	0	47
5. Hank Aaron 2/5/34	20	12	10	DNP	42
6. Willie Mays 5/6/31	18	8	6	DNP	32
7. Willie McCovey 1/10/38	12	15	1	DNP	28
8. Enos Slaughter 4/27/16	2	5	4	6	17
9. Al Kaline 12/19/34	13	DNP	DNP	DNP	13
Luke Appling 4/2/07	8	0	5	0	13
11. Frank Robinson 8/31/35	9	3	DNP	DNP	12
Walker Cooper 1/8/15	7	2	3	DNP	12
13. Mickey Vernon 4/22/18	8	3	0	DNP	11
14. Ty Cobb 12/18/86	4	5	1	DNP	10
15. Jimmy Dykes 11/10/96	7	1	2	DNP	10
Ron Fairly 7/12/38	10	DNP	DNP	DNP	10

DNP — Did not play
xx — Tied for league lead

19

FAST STARTERS, SLOW LEARNERS AND LATE FLOPS

Most Big Hitters, like other ballplayers, hit few if any home runs their first season or two in the big leagues, then start finding the range. In mid-career, their late 20s and early 30s, they attain the peak of their power. Toward the end of their playing days they tail off. Duke Snider's home run profile is almost a classic example of this pattern (see chart).

Some sluggers don't fit the mold, however. They hit the ground pounding.

Fast Starters

Ralph Kiner led the National League in four-baggers in the first post-war year of 1946, also his rookie season. He pumped 23 out. The next year, at age 25, he whacked 51 and tied the 34-year-old veteran John Mize for the title.

Joe DiMaggio and Eddie Mathews weren't a bit bothered by rookie awe or the Sophomore Jinx either. Joltin' Joe broke in with 29 long belts for the Yankees in 1936 and led the Bronxmen to their second of four consecutive pennants in 1937 with 46 league-leading homers. Mathews mashed 25 as

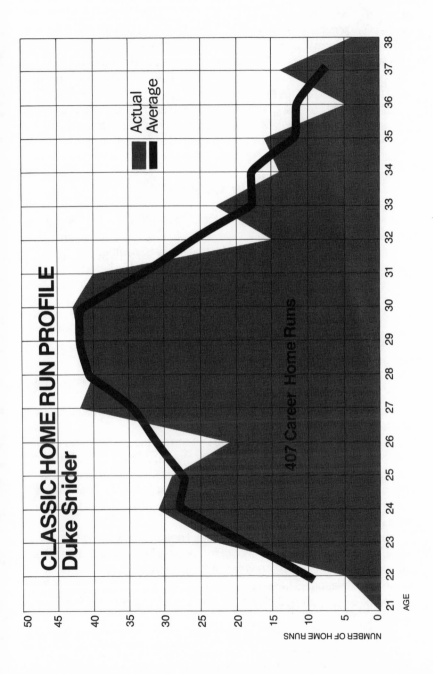

CLASSIC HOME RUN PROFILE
Duke Snider

Actual
Average

407 Career Home Runs

NUMBER OF HOME RUNS

AGE

a 1952 Braves rookie and followed with 47 to lead the league in '53. The respective second-year exploits of these two Big Hitters were their best home run performances ever.

Wally Berger and Frank Robinson each cracked 38 homers in their initial campaigns. Al Rosen, after three "false starts" in '47, '48 and '49, hit 37 to lead the AL in his first full season (1950).

Others who got going with a bang in their first complete seasons included Rudy York (35 in '37), Ted Williams (31 in '39), Richie Allen (29 in '64), Reggie Jackson (29 in '68), Orlando Cepeda (25 in '58) and Billy Williams (25 in '61).

Slow Learners

Some other eventual Big Hitters, on the other hand, took a long time to get untracked.

Hank Sauer was 29 years old before he finally blossomed into a BH. He first glimpsed major league pitching for the Reds in 1941, came up a few more times in '42, went back to "farming" in Syracuse in '43 and then spent '44 and most of '45 in the military, coming up a few times at the end of the last war year. His major league homer total through three partial seasons was an unimpressive five. He then paid his dues for two more years back in Syracuse. His 50 homers there in 1947 finally convinced the Reds' front office that Hank was ready for the big time.

He spanked 35 beyond the outfielders' clutches in '48. Sauer's reward for this fine effort was to be traded to the Cubs in '49.

Harmon Killebrew, George Foster and Gorman Thomas were also slow starters, or late bloomers, as the case may be.

Killebrew first donned a big league uniform for the old Senators in 1954 at the tender age of 18. He had 13 official plate appearances and no home runs. For the next four years, he got a few more chances (never as many as 100 at-bats, however) and managed 11 HR. Finally, after five "partials," and still young at 23, he got rolling. In his first full year, 1959, he tied for the AL lead with 42 four-masters.

Foster was in and out of major league lineups for six years, from 1969 through 1974 with the Giants and Reds. He had 27 NL homers during these trying times. Then, in 1975, nearing his 26th birthday, he finally showed his strength, powering 26 baseballs over the wall. Two years later, in 1977, he uncorked 52 long pops, the most for a National Leaguer since Kiner's 54 in 1949.

Thomas had the uninspiring totals of 2, 2, 10 and 8 HR's in 668 plate appearances for the Brewers from 1973 through '76. Like Sauer before him, he had to spend a lot of time in this period honing his home run cut in

Neither rookie awe nor the sophomore jinx bothered Big Hitter EDDIE MATHEWS (Braves, 1952-53).

Courtesy Atlanta Braves

the hinterlands. In Sacramento in '74, the notorious short porch there helped him crash 51 homers. But his sub-.200 batting and anemic homer totals in '75–76 in the bigs found him back in the minors (Spokane) for the entire 1977 season. There, with 36 homers and a .322 BA, the Brewers decided Thomas at long last had it right. So, in 1978, approaching age 28 and after managing just 22 homers total spanning five AL seasons, Stormin' Gorman clubbed 32 roundtrippers for the big club and got that up to a league-leading 45 in '79.

The early-career frustrations of Hank, Harmon, George and Gorman and their ilk beg some questions. Did they just not have HRs in their bats in their younger years? Or was it the old chicken-and-egg controversy? They didn't hit homers because they didn't get to play regularly or they didn't get to play because they didn't produce?

Late Flops

The leading late-flop candidates among Big Hitters are Harry Davis, Rogers Hornsby and Chuck Klein.

Davis led the AL in home runs for four straight years, 1904 through 1907. Sure, it didn't take all that many four-base wallops to win the honor in those days. Davis beat the competition with the funny figures of 10, 8, 12 and 8. But he was consistent in banging balls for the distance from 1901 through 1909, averaging more than seven a year. Then, for his last eight campaigns, he hit the grand total of two, including none at all for his final six seasons. Of course, he seldom came to the plate in the twilight of his career. Yet, that string of naughts at the end of his record looks mighty curious for a player who qualified as a Big Hitter in the early years of the Junior Circuit.

The 33-year-old Rogers Hornsby cracked 39 HR for the pennant-winning Cubs in 1929, then hit only 24 more over the next eight years. Here again, the Rajah didn't play too much, coming up to the dish an average of less than 100 times a season.

Maybe Davis and Hornsby just wore out. Davis played 22 years total and Hornsby was active during 23 campaigns. Davis played no more after age 44 and Hornsby took his last cuts at 41.

Klein was essentially a fast starter and a late flubber. Chuck and the supposedly souped-up ball arrived in the NL at about the same time. Klein clubbed 11 homers in his coming-out year, 1928, following that with 43 in 1929. That was the league record at the time and proved to be his career high. By 1937, he was essentially through as a legitimate HR threat, though he kept playing into 1944. Chuck's homer-hitting profile looks decidedly different from the Snider "normal" (see chart).

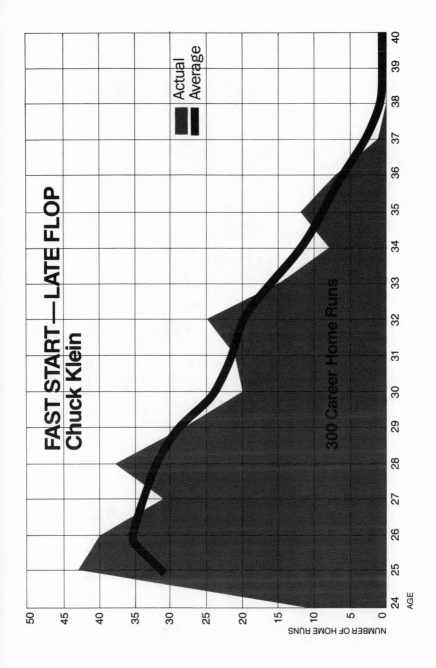

FAST START—LATE FLOP
Chuck Klein

300 Career Home Runs

Actual
Average

NUMBER OF HOME RUNS

AGE

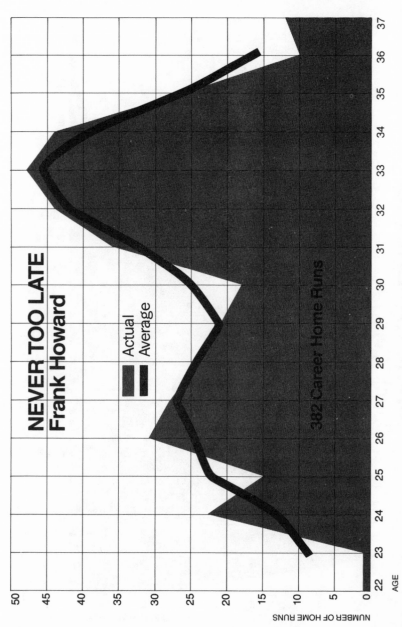

NEVER TOO LATE
Frank Howard

Actual
Average

382 Career Home Runs

NUMBER OF HOME RUNS

AGE

The average on the charts is a three-year moving average that "smooths out the kinks" caused by year-to-year differences in performance. For instance, Snider hit 31 HR at age 24, 29 at age 25 and 21 at age 26, a total of 81. For the three years, that averages out to 27 HR at age 25. Next, his HR for ages 25-27 (29+21+42) are totaled (92) and averaged (92/3) for age 26 (30.7) and so on.

A Late Bloomer

Frank Howard, on the other hand, was an early disappointment and a later sensation. Hondo was one of those big boffers who always had "great potential." He put together a Big Hitter year in his fifth season with the Dodgers, belting 31 and hitting .296 at age 26. But the management got restless as they watched his home run totals and BA decline the next two years (to 28 and .273, then 24 and .226). Thus he was put on the trading block and left the City of Angels in favor of the Nation's Capital. There his average perked up, but his big bat still slumbered. As far as the Big Hit was concerned, his output dwindled to 21 in 1965 and 18 the following year. Then, at long last, at age 31, Frank started nailing pitches like everyone always thought somebody 6'7" and 265 pounds could. He became the Capital Punisher, parking 36, 44, 48 and again 44 in a four-year span, twice leading the league. His HR profile is almost the mirror image of Klein's (see chart).

Too Hard to Classify

Roy Sievers' record is too hard to classify. He had a fine rookie season but, unlike DiMaggio and Mathews, endured the sophomore jinx (for four years!) before he finally overcame adversity and became a consistent player.

In Roy's rookie year, 1949, he lofted 16 homers and batted .306 in 140 games for the Browns. When it came time to pass out the American League Rookie of the Year Award, the experts looked over the freshmen and said, "Roy, go to the head of the class!" But the next year, his grades fell way off and in succeeding seasons he battled injuries and almost flunked out.

In 1950, his HR production dropped to 10 and his BA plummeted 68 points to .238 as he played in 113 games. In 1951, after 31 miserable games with one HR and a .225 BA, he was shuffled off to San Antonio. But there he suffered a shoulder separation making a tumbling catch and was reinjured during early spring training. He didn't play again until September, 1952. During 1953, he started a comeback, playing 92 games, connecting for eight homers and batting .270. When the Brownies pulled up stakes in St. Louis after the '53 season and moved east to Baltimore, Roy wasn't with them. He played about 40 miles south, having been traded to the Senators in the off-season. In 1954, Sievers finally turned in his learner's permit and graduated from the sophomore ranks. He got pretty good marks in his first year with Washington, 24 homers and a .232 average in 145 games. From then on, he was an outstanding student of the game. He really became an upperclassman in 1957 when he authored 42 home runs to lead the league. He also led in RBI, batted .301, and hit six homers in six straight games.

Before school was out for Sievers in 1965, nearing age 39, he had guided 318 balls beyond the walls and tested out at 71 points in the N-ratings,ranking him in the top 50.Through perseverance, Roy had at last vindicated those who recognized his early promise.

20

FAMOUS FIRSTS (AND LASTS)

Bobby Bonds hit a grand slam in his first major league game. Willie Mays' first big league hit was a homer, after he had gone 0 for 12 in his first three games.

Bob Nieman hit four-baggers in his first two at bats in the majors. Gene Tenace hit home runs in his first two World Series at bats. Jim Palmer got his first pitching victory and first homer in one game.

Interesting as these and other "firsts" are, "lasts" are sometimes ignored, but often no less interesting.

Mel Ott homered in his first World Series game in 1933 and also in his last in '37. Ty Cobb hit his first major league home run when he was 19 years old and his last when he was 41. He is the only player to hit home runs both as a teenager and over age 40.

Ted Williams hit a boomer in his last major league at bat. Early-era blaster Gavvy Cravath, managing the Phils in 1920, put himself into the lineup as a pinch-hitter, hit a three-run homer which won the game 3–0. It was his only four-master of the season and the last of his career.

Only once did brothers hit successive homers in the majors. Lloyd and Paul Waner, both Hall of Famers, did it and it was Lloyd's last round-tripper in the bigs.

Tommy Harper hit a homer in the top of the 20th inning for Seattle and it looked like the long blow had finally ended this double-overtime struggle. But Joe LaHoud, it turned out, delivered the last blast. His two-run home run in the bottom of the 20th was the winning hit for the Red Sox.

It took almost as long until a homer broke up a game in 1915. Vic Saier's four-base hit in the 19th inning rewarded the Cubs with a 4–3 victory over the Dodgers. Saier's four-master made pitcher Zip Zabel a winner after 18⅓ innings of relief work, the longest such performance in major league history. Zabel came on with two out in the first inning; Jeff Pfeffer pitched the whole game for Brooklyn.

Lou Gehrig hit his 493rd and last four-base wallop on September 27, 1938, 15 years to the day after he whacked his first.

Some players, notably pitchers, did the first and last in one swing of the bat:

Hoyt Wilhelm helped himself to win his first major league game (in relief) with a homer in his first time at bat. The knuckle baller appeared in 1,070 games over the next 20 years and won or saved a lot of them, but he never hit another homer. Pitcher Mickey Lolich's lone big league homer was clubbed in a World Series game. Pitcher Joe Niekro's only major league four-base wallop to date was spanked off his brother, Phil. Joe was the winning pitcher that "first and last" day in 1976.

Talk about that 20-inning Seattle-Boston bash, how about this one? Jack Reed, a substitute Yankee outfielder, hit a homer in the 22nd inning of a 1962 game to win it. It was the latest inning for any major league HR and also Reed's first and only major league home run.

Babe Ruth, always looming larger than life, it seems, had several firsts and lasts worthy of note. He hit the first HR in Yankee Stadium and the first in an All-Star game. He was the first to hit as many as 30, 40, 50 or 60 in a season (his 54 in 1920 surpassed his own previous high of 29). He was also the first to reach the 200, 300, 400, 500, 600 and 700 HR-in-a-lifetime marks.

Ruth's first minor league home run was also his last as a minor leaguer. Pitching for Providence in the International League in 1914, he allowed Toronto only one hit and contributed to the 9–0 whitewashing with the three-run clout.

The closing chapter of the swat king's career is not really summed up in his last home run (that was dramatic enough, however), but in his last season. That year, 1935, was both sensational and pitiful.

Released from the Yankees, 40 years old, ravaged by 20 years of pitching, hitting, over-indulgence and the relentless glare of the public spotlight, no team wanted him but the woebegone Braves.

Rising to the occasion, one more time as it were, he "broke in" in the NL

Knuckleballer HOYT WILHELM hit his first and only homer in a 21-year career while he was collecting his first of 123 relief pitching victories (Giants, 1952).

with a flourish by punching one out against Carl Hubbell. (This was the same screwball artist who just a year before struck out five famed American Leaguers in a row in the All-Star game, beginning with Ruth.) The Braves beat the Giants that day, 4–2 in Braves Field, as Ruth also singled.

The next dramatic day came more than a month later, on May 25. The Braves were playing in Pittsburgh. Ruth smashed three homers and a single for more total bases than he had ever amassed in a game before. His third HR of the day was his sixth of the year, the 714th and last of his career and cleared the right-field roof of Forbes Field (no one had ever done that).

But the Braves lost that day, as they did on most other days. George Herman "Babe" Ruth, batting .181 and with no extra-base hits besides the six homers, gave it up a few days later. With and without the Babe, the Braves that year had one of the worst campaigns in baseball history, winning 38 and losing 115, as they finished deep in the cellar, 61½ games behind the Chicago Cubs.

The mighty Yankees, the club that in the end turned its back on a legend, didn't win either. Sure, they wound up second only three games behind the Tigers, but few ever remember who finished second. Would Ruth have made the difference?

21

SHORT TAKES ON LONG HITS

With a Few Homers More . . .

The 1982 AL Champion Milwaukee Brewers made a run at the 1961 Yankees' team record of 240 HR, but wound up 24 short of the mark. With a few homers more, Harvey's Wallbangers (Harvey Kuenn was their manager) could have caused several pages of this book to be rewritten.

Center fielder Gorman Thomas had 39 big hits. One more would have given him 40 and the league lead outright, thus adding 15 points in the N-ratings, vaulting him into the 37th spot instead of 42nd.

MVP Shortstop Robin Yount blasted 29. He whacked two in the final, winner-take-all shootout with the Orioles to reach that mark. One more would have given the Brewers "Four Masters" — four players with 30 or more HR — as only the '77 Dodgers have ever managed. (Besides Gorman Thomas and Robin Yount, Ben Oglivie and Cecil Cooper clubbed more than 30 each.)

Leadoff man Paul Molitor finished with 19 long belts. One more would have given the True Blue Brew Crew six players with 20 or more HR, accomplished only by three other teams. (Catcher Ted Simmons would have been the other member of the Super Six.)

The Babe Out-Foxx-ed

Jimmie Foxx had the longest string of Big Hitter seasons of any ballplayer. He crashed 30 or more 12 years in a row, from 1929 through 1940. Twice in that span he lifted 50 or more (58 in 1932 and 50 in 1938) and thrice he touched off 40 or more.

The Babe's big bellyache in 1925 prevented him from reeling off 14 consecutive 30-and-up seasons. Illness laid him low in spring training, he underwent surgery for an intestinal abscess and didn't get into the lineup until June. He wound up with a still-respectable 25 homers. Otherwise, he blasted 30 or more every year from 1920 through 1933. In those 14 years, he rapped 60 once, more than 50 three times and 40 or more seven times.

Other players with outstanding strings of 30-plus homer hitting: Lou Gehrig and Eddie Mathews, nine in a row each and Mickey Mantle, eight in succession.

This Will Give You the Willies

It seems as though almost every Willie who ever played the game has made a reputation on the Big Hit. Willie Mays is No. 3 in the N-ratings. His teammate, Willie McCovey is No. 16. Willie Stargell ranks 19th and hit his team's only three HR in a World Series. Willie Wilson whacked five inside-the-park homers one year. Willie Aikens knocked four home runs in a World Series. Willie Horton circled the bases 325 times in his career.

Willie Randolph smacked a four-bagger to make his team victorious in the 1981 AL playoffs, then popped two more in the World Series, after hitting only two in the regular season. Willie McGee had a similar performance the following autumn. He slapped the only round-tripper in the NL playoff series and could have had a second (inside-the-park) if he had only heeded his third base coach. McGee followed with two HR in the Series, after driving only four in the regular season.

Willie Davis had 182 career homers and his 2,000th major league hit was a home run. Willie (Puddin' Head) Jones ripped one of the five homers that the Phils collected in one inning of a 1949 game against the Reds. Willie Smith, it would seem, made a living busting pinch-hit homers. Willie Upshaw got rolling in 1982 by slugging 21 home runs at age 25.

Willie Crawford, a Dodger outfielder for 12 years and Willie Miranda, an AL shortstop for nine, are a couple of the only Willies I can think of whose names weren't much associated with Big Hits. Crawford had 74 lifetime and Miranda only six. Willie Hernandez is a relief pitcher who seldom bats (three times up in 1982, for instance) and has never hit a home run in the majors.

Now Wee Willie Keeler didn't make his name by hitting for the distance either, but he must surely be the lifetime record holder for players his size (5'4" and 140 pounds) and he hit more homers (34) than many larger players.

Finally, wasn't it Willie Wonka who lofted one over a chocolate factory, or is that another story?

When 2 HR Beat 19 SO

It was mid-September, 1969. The Amazin' Mets were on a roll that would take them right on through the World's Championship. Not even Steve Carlton's 19 strikeouts could deter the Shea Stadium group. Ron Swoboda banged two HR to drive in all the Mets' runs in a 4–3 victory over the defending champion Cardinals, despite Carlton's performance.

A year later, Carlton was victimized by the Reds' Johnny Bench who solved him for three straight four-base hits. Steve also surrendered the first HR hit in the new Olympic Stadium in Montreal in 1977. Maybe it was these embarrassing experiences which locked Steve's jaw (he hasn't spoken to the press in years).

Jack and Rosy Rise Again

In the 1923 World Series, the Giants were down to their last out and trailing the Yankees 3–2 in games and 6–4 on the scoreboard. Jack Bentley, a good hitting pitcher who played some first base later in his career, was sent up to hit for fellow pitcher Rosy Ryan. Jack grounded out to end the Series.

So? So the next year, John McGraw, having skippered the Giants to their fourth straight pennant, let Jack and Rosy bat for themselves in the Series and both hit home runs. Ryan came on in relief of Hugh McQuillan in game three, aided his own cause with a homer and gained the win in the 6–4 game against the Senators. In game five, it was Bentley's turn to provide the heroics. He started the game, won 6–2 and connected for a two-run HR. This time McQuillan relieved him and picked up the save.

It was the only time in Series history that two pitchers on the same club hit balls out. But alas, the Giants dropped the seventh and final game. The losing pitcher: Jack Bentley, in relief of McQuillan.

Doing Double Duty

Speaking of homers by pitchers in Series play, here's the complete list:

Player, Team	All Series				Year Hit HR(s)
	AB	H	HR	BA	
Jim Bagby (Sr.), Indians	6	2	1	.333	1920
Rosy Ryan, Giants	4	1	1	.250	1924
Jack Bentley, Giants	12	5	1	.417	1924
Jesse Haines, Cardinals	9	4	1	.444	1926
Bucky Walters, Reds	10	2	1	.200	1940
Lew Burdette, Braves	17	1	1	.059	1958
Mudcat Grant, Twins	8	2	1	.250	1965
Jose Santiago, Red Sox	2	1	1	.500	1967
Bob Gibson, Cardinals	17	3	2	.176	1967, '68
Mickey Lolich, Tigers	12	3	1	.250	1968
Dave McNally, Orioles	16	2	2	.125	1969, '70
Ken Holtzman, A's	12	4	1	.333	1974

Bagby's homer came in a memorable game when two other "firsts" were recorded: Elmer Smith hit the first Series grand slam and Bill Wambsganss turned an unassisted triple play.

Walters was the only pitcher to homer in a 32-year span of 180 games. By contrast, six pitchers hit eight home runs in the 10-year period 1965–74 in a span of 55 games.

Lolich's was the first and only major league HR he ever hit. McNally's 1970 homer was a slam; his only two Series hits both were for the distance. For three others, Ryan, Burdette and Santiago, their homer was the only time they hit safely in Series play.

Homers-Only Hitters

Non-pitchers whose only Series hit(s) were homers:

Player, Team	All Series				Year Hit HR(s)
	AB	H	HR	BA	
Hank Majeski, Indians	6	1	1	.167	1954
Chuck Essegian, Dodgers	3	2	2	.667	1959
Ed Kranepool, Mets	7	1	1	.143	1969
Jim Mason, Yankees	1	1	1	1.000	1976

Breaking in the Ballparks

If Yankee Stadium is the house that Ruth built, it was properly christened. In the first game played there, April 18, 1923, the Sultan homered. A record crowd of 72,400 watched Ruth lead the Yankees to victory over the Red Sox.

Henry Aaron also helped dedicate a new ballpark, but he did not ingratiate himself with the home folks. In the first game played at Riverfront Stadium in Cincinnati in 1970, Aaron connected for a first-inning homer and the visiting Braves went on to crush the Reds, 8–2. But the Reds went on to fly a pennant from the new park that year. Aaron must have had a real liking for Riverfront. Four years later, in the earliest opening day in major league history, in Riverfront, before 52,000 fans, Aaron socked a three-run blast his first time up. It was his 714th, tieing Ruth. What's more, Aaron and the visiting Braves won a thriller, 7–6 in 11 innings.

Have a Good Day

Who has had the biggest Big Hitter game? The jury is still out on that question. It all depends on how you look at it.

Several big leaguers have slammed four balls for the distance in one game. When Joe Adcock added a double to his four, four-baggers, he set the single-game total bases record of 18. Jim Bottomley went six for six in a game, including two homers, and batted in 12 runs. That's a single-game RBI record. Tony Lazzeri came close to that with 11 RBI and some might say he topped it, because he had three homers and a triple and two of the long bangers were grand slams (and he was the No. 8 batter in the lineup)!

Willie Mays and Daryl Spencer of the Giants came on like gang busters in a 16–9 romp over the Dodgers in 1958. Their "line score":

	HR	3B	2B	1B	RBI	TB
Mays	2	2	0	1	4	15
Spencer	2	1	1	0	6	13
Totals	4	3	1	1	10	28

Pound for pound, Freddie Patek, 5'5" and 148, may have had the most impressive game when he punched three HR and a double.

Most of the big individual effort games are part of lopsided laughers for the players' club. For example, Lazzeri's great game helped the Yanks stomp the A's 25–2. But the Phillies needed every one of Mike Schmidt's four HR and a single for eight RBI, as they edged the Cubs 18–16 in 10 innings in a 1976 contest.

Poosh 'Em Up TONY LAZZERI had a great game with two grand slams, another homer and triple as he drove home 11 runs in a 25-2 laugher (Yankees, 1936).

As for big days, Nate Colbert must be out in front. He had five HR and two singles in a double bill, good for 13 RBI and 22 total bases as the Padres swept the Braves, 9–0 and 11–7.

Four by Fours

Three Philadelphia National League players have hit four four-baggers in one game, each exactly 40 years apart: Ed Delahanty in 1896, Chuck Klein in 1936 and Mike Schmidt in 1976. Klein's clouts were the first in the league in the 20th Century; Schmidt's the last recorded in either major league.

Another 19th Century National Leaguer, Boston's Bobby Lowe, is credited with being the first to get four Big Hits in one major league game, in 1894. It wasn't until 1932 that an American Leaguer, Lou Gehrig, could crack four big smackers in one game.

The 20th Century four by fours:

1932—Lou Gehrig, Yankees
1936—Chuck Klein, Phillies
1948—Pat Seerey, White Sox
1950—Gil Hodges, Dodgers
1954—Joe Adcock, Braves
1959—Rocky Colavito, Indians
1961—Willie Mays, Giants
1976—Mike Schmidt, Phillies

Only one of the eight, Pat Seerey, does not rate as a Big Hitter. The others are all in the top 70 of the N-ratings.

Knock Three Times

Johnny Mize holds the major league record for most times hitting three home runs in a game. Twice in 1938 and again in 1940 he knocked three out in one game for the Cardinals. In 1947 as a Giant and in 1950 in a Yankee uniform he turned the three-homers-in-a-game hat trick again. Lou Gehrig holds the AL record; four different times he hit three homers in one game. Six other players besides Mize had two three-homer games in one year.

Two, three-HR games in one year:

1938—Johnny Mize, Cardinals
1940—Johnny Mize, Cardinals
1947—Ralph Kiner, Pirates
1957—Ted Williams, Red Sox
1961—Willie Mays, Giants
1971—Willie Stargell, Pirates
1979—Dave Kingman, Cubs
1982—Doug DeCinces, Angels

To be Young and Playing in Brooklyn

Playing in his hometown, for the home team and in his home park, 17-year-old Tommy Brown hit a home run in Ebbets Field, Brooklyn, home of the Dodgers, in 1945. The youngest player ever to hit a major league round-tripper, teenaged Tommy was already playing in his second season that war year (he came up at age 16). He bopped the ball off of 30-year-old Preacher Roe of the Pirates. "The Preacher man" became Tommy's teammate in 1948. Roe had his best years with Brooklyn, closing out his career there in 1954. Brown was in the majors nine years, hit 31 homers and never played in more than 89 games in a season. At age 25, when many a ballplayer is just getting his start in the bigs, Brown was all through.

Thunderbolt and Lightfoot

Five players have combined Big Hit seasons with what might be called Big Steal seasons (30 or more stolen bases), but in no case did they lead the league in both departments. Bobby Bonds thundered and lightninged his way to five of the 10 such performances, in both leagues and with five different teams. In his Big Hit-Big Steal seasons, he never led in either category.

Year	Player, Team	HR	SB
1922	Ken Williams, Browns	39x	37
1956	Willie Mays, Giants	36	40x
1957	Willie Mays, Giants	35	38x
1963	Hank Aaron, Braves	44xx	31
1969	Bobby Bonds, Giants	32	45
1970	Tommy Harper, Brewers	31	38
1973	Bobby Bonds, Giants	39	43
1975	Bobby Bonds, Yankees	32	30
1977	Bobby Bonds, Angels	37	41
1978	Bobby Bonds, White Sox-Rangers	31	43

x — League Leader
xx — Tied for Lead

Records to Go

Here are some major league long-ball records which have never been achieved, through 1983:

No. HR

756—by one player in his career
503—off one pitcher in his career
241—by one team in a season
62—by one player in a season
57—by a National League player in a season
47—off one pitcher in a season
39—by a rookie in a season
33—by a designated hitter in a season
30—by a player 40 years old or older
19—by one player in one month
13—by one team in a Series
12—by two teams in one game
11—by a team other than the Yankees in a Series
10—by a pitcher in a season
9—by one player in nine consecutive games
8—by a National League pitcher in a season
7—by a pinch hitter in a season
6—by one player in a doubleheader or a Series
5—by one player in one game
4—by one player in a Series game
3—by one player in an All-Star game
2—grand slams by one player in one inning
1—inside-the-park grand slam by a pitcher in extra innings
0—by both teams in a league championship (playoff) series

Home Run Fun

Joe Garagiola wrote *Baseball Is a Funny Game*. Home run action has provided its share of the mirth.

The mercurial Jimmy Piersall once amused himself and the spectators (but not baseball brass) by running the bases backwards, so tickled was he at putting away his 100th career conk.

It may have been pretty funny to watch Tony Conigliaro walk slowly around the diamond after he jerked one out. It wasn't so funny as far as Tony was concerned, however. He wrenched his back swinging, proceeded painfully around the horn to home, then left the game in agony.

Cesar Cedeno of the Astros stepped to the dish in the fifth inning of a game against the Dodgers with the bags jammed. He lifted a 200-foot fly that dropped when the Dodgers' second baseman and right fielder collided chasing it. Cedeno circled the sacks for a grand slam.

Tim McCarver didn't have such good fortune on the Nation's most glorious birthday, July 4, 1976. He likewise came up with all bases occupied and knocked one into the stands. But the runner on first for the Phils, Garry Maddox, wasn't so sure it wouldn't be caught. He started for second, then turned back toward first. While retracing his steps, McCarver met and passed him and was called out for passing a runner. Scratch one grand slam. It was still a happy day for the team, though. The Phils beat the Pirates 10–5.

During the last year of World War II, 1945, a funny thing happened in Washington. Joe Kuhel hit the only four-bagger for the Senators in their home ball park, Griffith Stadium, and it was an inside-the-park blow at that.

A funny thing about the Braves' Brett Butler (not to be confused with Rhett Butler, who also had Atlanta connections): he batted 581 times in the majors before getting a four-base hit. Then he homered in two consecutive games.

This book does not deal with minor league HR, but this account in *This Date in Baseball History* strikes me as too funny to pass up: "June 15, 1902—Corsicana defeated Texarkana 51–3 in a Texas League game played in nearby Ennis, because of the Sunday blue laws. In this game, Nig Clarke of Corsicana took advantage of a small park to hit eight home runs. Some telegraph operators, thinking there was a mistake, reported the score as 5–3."

In a Texas League game played early in 1983, the long-standing record of 54 runs scored in the Corsicana-Texarkana game was broken when El Paso bonked Beaumont 35–21 (56 combined runs). The two teams crashed nine homers. The next night the two teams "settled down," scoring only 33 runs as Beaumont won, 20–13.

If you don't think baseball is a funny game, answer this one: What other sport can you name where the defense controls the ball?

22

BABE RUTH, THE TIEBREAKER

At the end of the 1919 season, Babe Ruth and Cy Williams each had 49 career HR. Gavvy Cravath was the World Leader with 118 (counting 20th Century HR only). But Cravath had only one more season left and hit only one more boomer. Ruth and Williams went on to be the first in their respective leagues to register 200 lifetime four-baggers. It took Williams until 1926 to accomplish that; Ruth hit the 200 mark in 1923. Ruth broke his 1919 tie with Williams in one year and never looked back. Baltimore Babe's 54 long swats sent him over the 100 mark in 1920 (it took Williams until 1922 to do it).

In 1927, when Ruth racked up his 60, Williams, approaching his 40th birthday, cracked half as many, 30, but enough to gain him a tie with Hack Wilson for the NL season lead. Rogers Hornsby also went over the 200 barrier in 1927, the third major leaguer to do so.

At the end of the 1928 season, Ruth had just about doubled the output of both Cy and Rogers (470 to 246 and 238, respectively). In following seasons, Lou Gehrig and Jimmie Foxx would also leave the NLers far behind.

Mel Ott was the first to collect 300 career homers in the NL. He reached that goal in 1937 and was the National's career HR king for almost 30 years. Willie Mays took over in 1966 and Hank Aaron succeeded him in 1972.

Ruth has held the AL career HR leadership every year for more than 60 years.

Here are the career HR leaders year by year in each major league (20th century HR only):

NATIONAL LEAGUE			AMERICAN LEAGUE		
1901	Sam Crawford	16	1901	Nap Lajoie	14
1902	Sam Crawford	19	1902	Socks Seybold	24
1903	Jimmie Sheckard	24	1903	Buck Freeman	36
1904	Jimmie Sheckard	25	1904	Buck Freeman	43
1905	Jimmie Sheckard	28	1905	Buck Freeman	46
1906	Jimmie Sheckard	29	1906	Harry Davis	49
1907	Jimmie Sheckard	30	1907	Harry Davis	57
1908	Jimmie Sheckard	32	1908	Harry Davis	62
1909	Jimmie Sheckard	33	1909	Harry Davis	66
1910	Jimmie Sheckard	38	1910	Harry Davis	67
1911	Frank Schulte	48	1911–14	Harry Davis	68
1912	Frank Schulte	60	1915–16	Harry Davis & Sam Crawford	68
1913	Frank Schulte	69	1917	Sam Crawford	70
1914	Sherry Magee	75	1918	Sam Crawford & Frank Baker	70
1915	Frank Schulte	86	1919	Frank Baker	80
1916	Frank Schulte	91	1920	Babe Ruth	103
1917	Gavvy Cravath	96	1921	Babe Ruth	162
1918	Gavvy Cravath	104	1922	Babe Ruth	197
1919	Gavvy Cravath	116	1923	Babe Ruth	238
1920–22	Gavvy Cravath	117	1924	Babe Ruth	284
1923	Cy Williams	149	1925	Babe Ruth	309
1924	Cy Williams	173	1926	Babe Ruth	356
1925	Cy Williams	186	1927	Babe Ruth	416
1926	Cy Williams	204	1928	Babe Ruth	470
1927	Cy Williams	234	1929	Babe Ruth	516
1928	Cy Williams	246	1930	Babe Ruth	565
1929	Rogers Hornsby	277	1931	Babe Ruth	611
1930	Rogers Hornsby	279	1932	Babe Ruth	652
1931	Rogers Hornsby	295	1933	Babe Ruth	686
1932	Rogers Hornsby	296	1934–83	Babe Ruth	708
1933–36	Rogers Hornsby	298			
1937	Mel Ott	306			
1938	Mel Ott	342			
1939	Mel Ott	369			
1940	Mel Ott	388			
1941	Mel Ott	415			
1942	Mel Ott	445			
1943	Mel Ott	463			

Year	Player	
1944	Mel Ott	489
1945	Mel Ott	510
1946–65	Mel Ott	511
1966	Willie Mays	542
1967	Willie Mays	564
1968	Willie Mays	587
1969	Willie Mays	600
1970	Willie Mays	628
1971	Willie Mays	646
1972	Hank Aaron	673
1973	Hank Aaron	713
1974–83	Hank Aaron	733

23

HOME RUNS TO REMEMBER

Home runs are usually dramatic. They're often decisive. Sometimes they're unforgettable. Following is a chronicle of some memorable home runs, hit in the World Series, playoffs, regular seasons and exhibitions. The narrative is in a "You Are There" format.

World Class Homers

The Series is loaded with home run lore; the fall classic is short, intense and watched even by casual fans, multiplying the drama and decisiveness of long swats, thus adding to their memorability.

1903—Jimmy Sebring hits a home run for Pittsburgh in the first Series game ever played. In the second game, Patsy Dougherty blasts two for the Red Sox.

1908—Cub Joe Tinker hits a two-run home run in the second game of the Series. It is the first four-bagger since Dougherty's two in 1903. The intervening 23 games were homerless.

1911—Home Run Baker gets his nickname for four-masters in two consecutive games. His two-run sixth inning base-clearer wins game two for the Athletics, 3–1; his solo sock sends game three into extra innings. The A's go on to win the Series over the Giants, four games to two.

1915—Harry Hooper hits his second HR of the game in the top of the ninth. It gives the Red Sox the deciding fifth-game Series win over the Phillies by a score of 5–4. Hooper hit only two four-baggers in 566 regular-season at bats.

1918—It's the last homerless Series ever played as the Red Sox win over the Cubs in six games. Only 19 runs are scored.

1920—Elmer Smith hits the first Series grand slam in the first inning of game five, as the Indians win 8–1 over Brooklyn.

1921—Babe Ruth hits his first Series round-tripper in game four, but the Yankees lose the game and eventually the Series to their intercity rivals, the Giants.

1923—Playing an all-Gotham Series for the third year in a row, but the first in two ballparks, Casey Stengel and Babe Ruth provide the theatrics in the first three games. Stengel's inside-the-park homer in the ninth inning of the opener at the new Yankee Stadium before a record Series crowd gives the Giants the win, 5–4. Stengel sprints around the bases with a shoe half off and plops safe on the plate. The Yankees think he's grandstanding. The Yanks have reason to be testy; it is their eighth consecutive Series loss to the Giants. The teams go cross-river to the Polo Grounds for the second encounter. Ruth explodes two four-baggers in successive times at bat, the first time that has ever been done. His clouts pace the Yanks' 4–2 win. The Bambino's longest drive of the day, however, goes to deepest center field in the ninth, where Stengel hauls it in. Switching back to Yankee Stadium for game three and another record attendance, Stengel's homer again wins it for the Giants, this time 1–0; he hits it into the right field bleachers over Ruth's head in the seventh inning. Casey, always the comic character, thumbs his nose at the Yankee bench as he rounds third. Commissioner Kenesaw Mountain Landis sees no humor in the gesture, chews out Stengel and fines him $50. The Series is odd in that the Giants lose all three games in their own ballpark and the Yankees win but one of three at home. But that one is the edge as the Yankees win their first Series, four games to two. Ruth homers in the sixth-game, 6–4 clincher (again at the Polo Grounds), making him the first to loft three round-trippers in one Series.

1924—Goose Goslin's three homers and "boy manager" Bucky Harris' pair pace the Senators to their first and only Series triumph, a seven-game struggle with the Giants. The Senators hit only 22 four-baggers in 154 regular season games, lowest in the major leagues, and follow with five in the seven Series games.

1925—Goslin smashes three HR for the second consecutive Series. Another Harris (Joe) also cracks three for the Senators and misses a fourth which would have tied the score in the ninth inning of game six. But a temporary screen in center field stops the ball and Harris' drive goes for a double. The Pirates win, 3–2 (the margin is Eddie Moore's solo homer) and also master the Nats in the next game to become the first team to come back from a 1–3 deficit (in a seven-game series) to win the World Championship. The most bizarre play, however, occurs in game three when Sam Rice robs Earl Smith of a homer, but not without some controversy. (See the Chapter on the "Third Dimension" for a discussion of Harris' and Smith's near misses.)

1926—Ruth hits three in one game.

1927—Ruth bangs the Series' two (and only) homers as the Yankees win all four games from the Pirates.

1928—The Babe turns the hat trick again; he has 10 hits, scores nine runs, bats .625 (a record) and leads the Bombers to a sweep of the Cardinals, avenging the seven-game loss to St. Louis in 1926.

1929—Mule Haas' two-run home run in the bottom of the ninth for the A's ties the fifth game of the Series, 2–2. A pair of following doubles produces the Series clincher over the Cubs.

1932—Does he or doesn't he? Does Ruth call his shot against Charlie Root in the third game, silencing the heckling of the Chicago players and fans? For sure, he hits two home runs in the game, as does Gehrig. The Cubs also have two long blasts. But the Yankees win, 7–5, and the next day put the Cubs out of their misery as Tony Lazzeri rams two out and Earle Combs also conks one for a four-game New York romp. Between them, Ruth and Gehrig score 15 runs and bat in 14. Ruth's "called shot" is his last Series homer.

1933—Mel Ott's homer in the top of the 10th is the deciding run of the last game of the Series for the Giants' 4-games-to-1 victory over the Senators.

1936—The Yankees' Tony Lazzeri pastes the second grand slam in Series history in game two. Bill Dickey adds a three-run clout as he and Lazzeri each bat in five runs. The Yanks bomb the Giants 18–4; the 18 runs by one team is a still-standing Series record. The mighty Yanks win the match in six games, crushing the Manhattan team 13–5 in the finale. It is the first of four consecutive championships for the Bronxmen.

1942—Whitey Kurowski's homer in the top of the ninth with Walker Cooper aboard gives the Cards the game, 4–2, and the Series, 4–1, over the Yankees.

1943—The Yanks, as they so often do, even the score with the Redbirds for the preceding year. Bill Dickey's two-run home run in the sixth inning makes the Yanks winners, 2–0 in the fifth game, and four games to one in the Classic.

1947—Yogi Berra of the Yankees hits the first pinch-hit HR in Series history in game three against the Dodgers.

1952—Mickey Mantle bashes his first of 18 Series homers, the record.

1953—The Yanks pound out nine HR to the Dodgers' eight as they take Brooklyn in six games. The 17 total is a record for two teams, one more than the same pair of combatants hit in '52 (but in seven games). The same two teams will equal the 17 total in two later Series (1955 and 1977).

1954—Dusty Rhodes wallops a three-run pinch-hit home run in the bottom of the 10th in game one to make the underdog Giants winners over the Indians. Rhodes comes in to pinch-hit again in game two, delivers a game-tying single and stays in the lineup, homering later. The Giants sweep the Series.

1955—Next year finally comes for the Dodgers. They outpound the Yankees, nine home runs to eight. Duke Snider smashes four for Dem Bums.

1956—Yogi Berra and Moose Skowron belt grand slams in a Series won by the Yankees over the Dodgers, four games to three. The Bronx Bombers have 12 homers in the Series, as they even the score for the Dodgers' seven-game '55 triumph. The Series is most memorable for Don Larsen's perfect game.

1960—Bill Mazeroski hits the most dramatic HR in Series history. The score is tied, 9–9, in the bottom of the ninth in the decisive seventh game when Maz steps up and drives the baseball over the left field wall in Pittsburgh's Forbes Field. This is the Series in which the Yankee wins are by scores of 16–3, 10–0 and 12–0; they have 10 homers to the Bucs' 4 and outscore them 55–27. But the Pirates win all the close ones.

1962—Chuck Hiller unloads the first NL slam in Series history, but the Yankees edge the Giants in seven games.

1966—The Orioles sweep the Series with the Dodgers. The last three games are shutouts and the last two are 1–0 scores, the only runs coming on homers by Paul Blair and Frank Robinson.

1967—The Red Sox sock three HR in the fourth inning of game six. The seat-reachers by Carl Yastrzemski, Reggie Smith and Rico Petrocelli help power the Bosox to an 8–4 victory. But the Cards take the Series in the final game.

1970—Oriole Pitcher Dave McNally does it all in game three. He pitches a complete game, a 9–3 victory, and smacks a grand slam. The Birds go on to win in five games over the Reds. There has not been a Series slam since. (Dave also hit a two-run homer in the '69 Series. That one wasn't so memorable. It was the fifth and deciding game and the Miracle Mets won it.)

1972—Gene Tenace hits home runs in his first two Series at bats, something never done before or since. He homers in the fourth and fifth games as well. He has nine RBI in the seven-game A's triumph over the Reds and bats .348. (Tenace had five HR in the regular season and batted .225. In the playoffs, he did not homer and batted .059.)

1973—The A's wait until the seventh game before homering. Then Bert Campaneris and Reggie Jackson each bash two-run blasts in the third inning. The A's final-game "plan" works as they whip the Mets 5–2.

1975—In what is called the most exciting World Series game ever, the Reds and Red Sox duke it out in Boston until late into the night. Pinch-hitter Bernie Carbo's three-run homer for the Sox ties the game in the eighth inning, 6–6. The Red Sox load the bases with nobody out in the 10th but don't score. In the 12th inning, Carlton Fisk sends a home run into the chill air to clinch the win for Boston. But the next day the Reds win the game by a 4–3 score and the Series by the same margin in games. A personal note: I will always remember that spine-tingling sixth game, not so much for what I witnessed but for what I *didn't* experience. Figuring I needed to be alert for work in the morning, I turned off the set and went to bed after the ninth inning. The next day, I regretted that sleepy-headed decision and have ever since. I missed some great drama and wasn't all that alert at work anyway.

1976—The Reds' Johnny Bench takes Yankee pitching downtown twice in the fourth and final game of the Series. Bench drives home five in the 7–2 win as the Big Red Machine rumbles to its second consecutive World Championship, after also sweeping the playoffs against the Phillies.

1977—Reggie Jackson cracks five HR, a Series record, and biffs three of them in the decisive sixth game, each on the first pitch. Only Ruth hit three in a Series game before. Jackson scores 10 runs and knocks in eight, batting .450.

1978—"Mr. October" does it again. Jackson paces the Big Apple team to its second straight six-game triumph over the Dodgers, his HR icing the final win. He has two homers, drives in eight runs and bats .391 for the Series. Reggie's combined playoff and Series performance: 4 HR, 14 RBI and a .417 BA in 10 games.

1979—Thirty-eight-year-old Willie Stargell unites the Pirates' "Family" as they recover from a 1–3 deficit to defeat the Orioles in seven games. His two-run homer paces the Pirates to the final-game victory. He whops all of his team's homers (three) and bats .400, earning the most valuable award. He was also the MVP of the NL playoffs and Co-MVP (with Keith Hernandez of the Cardinals) for the regular season. Willie's complete post-season stats: 17 hits, 5 homers, 13 RBI and a .415 batting average.

1980—The Royals' Willie Mays Aikens does something his illustrious namesake never did in a World Series: hit a home run. Willie (Aikens) hits not just one, but four, and is the only player to hit more than one HR in two different games in a single Series. Willie raps two two-run blasts in game one, but the Phils prevail, 7–6. He smacks two more in game four, with a happier result (Kansas City wins 5–3). In game three, Aikens' triple in the bottom of the 10th drives Willie Wilson home for a 4–3 KC victory. It is

Aikens' first major league triple. He winds up the Series with eight RBI and a .400 BA. But he doesn't do what Willie Mays did—lead his team to a Series triumph. The Phils eliminate the Royals in six games.*

Playoff Power

In 1969, each major league was expanded from 10 to 12 teams, East and West divisions were created in both the AL and NL and best-of-five playoff series begun between division leaders to determine each league champion. Before 1969, ties at the end of the regular season necessitated best-of-three playoff series in the National League in 1946, 1951, 1959 and 1962. The Dodgers were one of the teams in all four playoffs, but won only in '59. The American League opted for sudden-death, one-game playoffs to settle ties. It happened only in 1948 before the divisions were set up. Ties in the AL East in 1978 and the NL West in 1980 necessitated one-game divisional playoffs. The 1981 "split season" resulted in best-of-five divisional playoffs before the league championship series. Home runs have supplied a fair share of the thrills in the various playoff contests.

1948—In the first playoff in AL history, player-manager Lou Boudreau goes 4-for-4, including two HR as the Indians beat the Red Sox 8–3.

1951—Bobby Thomson hits the most dramatic and decisive home run ever. The Giants come from 13½ games behind the Dodgers in mid-August to tie for the top spot at season's end. In fact, the Dodgers must scramble on the final day of the regular season to get the tie. In a spine-tingler, Jackie Robinson hoists a 14th-inning HR for a 9–8 victory over the Phils. The crosstown rivals split the first two games of the best-of-three playoff and square off in the Polo Grounds for the finale. It is the bottom of the ninth and the Giants trail 4–1. They get some hits and score a run, making it 4–2 with two men on. Ralph Branca (No. 13!) relieves the Flatbush ace, Don Newcombe. Branca fires a strike past Thomson, The Flying Scot. The next pitch, however, is the whole season. Thomson knocks it out of the park. There is a stunned silence, then pandemonium. The Yankees thrash the Giants in the World Series (Thomson is a mediocre hitter) but all that is anticlimactic to the Miracle of Coogan's Bluff.

---

* *Footnote*: Willie Mays never hit a home run in a Series (in 71 AB), nor did Rogers Hornsby (49 AB), Hack Wilson (47 AB) or Ted Williams (25 AB), to mention a few Big Hitters who were Series "ohfors." Ernie Banks and Ralph Kiner didn't either—they never got a chance.

BOBBY THOMSON (arrow) attracts a crowd as he approaches home plate after hitting the most dramatic and decisive home run ever (Giants, 1951).

1970—Oh, those Oriole pitchers! McNally drilled a homer in the '69 Series and followed with a grand slam in the '70 Classic. Mike Cuellar hits a slammer in game one of the '70 playoffs against the Twins. Mike isn't around long enough to win the game, but the Birds go 6–0 against the Twins in the first two regularly-scheduled AL playoff series.

1971—The skies are thick with flying baseballs as the Pirates submerge the Giants in four games. The victorious Bucs crash eight HR, their opponents five. Bob Robertson, Pirate first baseman, is a one-man wrecking crew as he drills three out of Candlestick and adds a double to plate five runs in the Bucs' 9–4, second-game victory. Robertson cracks another homer in game three.

1973—Rusty Staub hammers three homers for the Mets, his only three hits of the series (in 15 AB). He has a solo shot in game two and one-run and two-run 'trippers in game three, both Mets triumphs over the Reds. The Mets emerge victors in five games.

1976—With the American League Championship Series tied in games, 2–2, the Royals' George Brett rattles a three-run HR in the eighth inning in Yankee Stadium to tie the game 6–6. Chris Chambliss strides to the plate in the bottom of the ninth and is soon trotting the bases following a circuit clout which makes the Yankees champions. Chambliss also has two hits, including a home run, and three RBI in the Yanks' third-game, 5–3 win.

1977—Ron Cey and Dusty Baker hit grand slams in each of the first two games of the NL playoffs. The first game is a loser for the Dodgers but they then reel off three in a row to oust the Phils. Baker also hits another homer, drives in eight runs in all and bats .357.

1978—In a playoff game BEFORE the AL Championship series, Bucky Dent's three-run home run sparks the Yankees to a 5–4 win over the Red Sox for the East Division championship. In the regular East vs. West playoff series, George Brett hammers three homers in one game for the Royals. But it's all in vain as KC loses its third straight playoff to the Yankees. Reggie Jackson slaps two into the stands for the Yanks, knocks in six runs and bats .462. In the NL playoffs, the Dodgers out-homer the Phils 8–5 in a four-game triumph for the Chavez Ravine team. The Phils lose their third consecutive playoff series in which they win only two games.

1980—The Phillies and Astros stage the most exciting playoff series ever contested, the Phillies finally prevailing in the maximum of five games. The last four contests are all extra-inning affairs. There is only one round-tripper, hit by Greg Luzinski of the Phils, in the entire 50 innings and combined 362 AB. That's a "homer average" of .003. In the American League playoffs, the Royals atone for the Yankees' 1976–77–78 domination. Brett again plays a prominent role. His three-run homer in the seventh inning of the third game overcomes a 2–1 deficit and the Royals sweep the Yanks, winning the finale 4–2.

1981—Rick Monday's ninth-inning, two-out homer gives the Dodgers the NL championship in Montreal, following a 3-games-to-2 Dodger victory over Houston for the West Divisional title, made necessary by the strike-interrupted "split season."

1982—Cardinal Rookie Willie McGee unleashes the short, three-game set's only HR in the ninth inning of the last game. Willie could have had the NL playoff's only *two* HR. His drive in the series opener gets by the Braves' outfielders. But he pulls up at third with the throw still nowhere near him. By the time he looks up, it is too late to score and he settles for a triple. As it turns out, in addition to the only HR, McGee also hits the only two triples in the St. Louis sweep.

Footnote: The leading homer hitters in Championship Series (playoffs) history through 1982 are Steve Garvey, seven; George Brett and Reggie Jackson, six each and Johnny Bench, Greg Luzinski, Sal Bando and Graig Nettles, five each.

Irregular Home Runs in Regular Seasons

It's no easy task to pick out the most memorable home runs in about 118,000 major league games played from 1901 through 1982. Here's a try:

1902—Pitcher Mike O'Neill of the Cardinals hits the first pinch-hit grand slam in a game against the Braves. No such hit was ever recorded for 19th century baseball.

1913—In a Memorial Day morning-afternoon double header, Harry Hooper of the Red Sox hits homers to lead off both a.m. and p.m. games; the second blast comes off of Walter Johnson of the Senators and stands up for a 1–0 Bosox win.

1919—The Red Sox' Babe Ruth previews the Big Hitter Era by shattering all the old home run records—Ned Williamson's all-time mark (27 for Chicago in 1884), Gavvy Cravath's modern major league record (24 for the Phillies in 1915) and Socks Seybold's American League high (16 for the Athletics in 1902)—by hitting 29. Ruth cracks four of his Big Hits with the bases filled, an AL season mark that endures for 40 years.

1920—The Big Hitter Era begins, "invented" by Ruth, now a New York Yankee. He personally out-homers every other major league team with the exception of the Phillies of cozy Baker Bowl and his Yankee teammates. The scoreboard reads Phils 64 HR, Yankees without Ruth 61, Ruth 54. The next best individual effort is by George Sisler, who manages all of 19 Big Hits. Cy Williams tops the NL with 15.

1921—Ruth breaks his own record, slugging 59 home runs.

1925—Kiki Cuyler of the Pirates hits eight inside-the-park home runs.

1927—Ruth's number 60 is significant. It's a two-run job in the eighth inning that rewards the Yankees with a 4–2 victory over the Senators. An added quirk of that historic event, paraphrased from *This Date in Baseball History*: "September 30—Pitcher Tom Zachary (surrenders Ruth's historic) blow and in the ninth inning gives way to pinch hitter Walter Johnson, making his final appearance as a player, who flies to Ruth."

1930—Hack Wilson sets the NL standard with 56 and drives in a still-unequaled 190 runs.

1932—Lou Gehrig bangs four circuit blows in a nine-inning game, a feat equaled several times; Johnny Frederick has six pinch-hit homers for the Dodgers. Chuck Klein ties for the NL lead in HR (38, the same number as Mel Ott hits) and also shows the way in stolen bases. It's the only time in history a player puts together power-speed championships.

Footnote: Lou Gehrig hit 23 regular-season grand slams, far more than Ruth or Aaron (tied for fifth with 16 each) and five more than runner-up Willie McCovey. The Iron Horse hit 10 Series homers, but none were with the bases loaded. Only one was a three-run job and six were solo blasts.

1937—Tiger rookie Rudy York, whose best position is first base, has a tough time finding a place in the lineup (Hank Greenberg is at first). He plays out of position at third base and catching. York finally gets a chance to play regularly in August, responds by slapping 18 homers, breaking Ruth's record of 17 in one month (Sept., 1927). The 18 are more than half York's season output of 35 long blasts.

1938—Gabby Hartnett hits his homer in the gloamin' for the Cubs. It is late in the season. The Cubs, who have been charging, are playing the Pirates, trailing them by 1/2 game in the standings. Darkness is settling in Wrigley Field, lightless then even as today. Score tied 5–5, two out in the bottom of the ninth; the umpires will call the game after this inning. Hartnett, the new manager, hits a two-strike pitch into the gloom. The Cubs win again the next day, breaking the Pirates' spirit and winning the pennant a few days hence.

1941—The Yankees homer in a record 25 consecutive games. Two other events, one thrilling, the other tragic, overshadow the team's homer run. The 25-game streak comes during Yankee Clipper Joe DiMaggio's unprecedented and unequaled record of hitting safely in 56 straight games, from May 15 through July 17, when he is finally stopped. A sad note punctuates the 56-game string and stirs memories of another matchless streak. Lou Gehrig dies on June 2, a few days before his 38th birthday. The incurable disease which eventually kills him forced him from the lineup barely two years earlier, after he had played in 2,130 consecutive games.

1944—The world is at war and the majors are populated by "Teenagers, Graybeards and 4-F's" (cf. Harrington Crissey's book by that title). The Browns and Tigers chug into the final day of the season in a flat-footed tie for first. The Brownies entertain the Yankees and the Tigers tangle with the Senators. In St. Louis, Chet Laabs powers home runs in both the fourth and fifth innings, both times behind Mike Kreevich singles. Vern Stephens' solo shot in the eighth ices the 5–2 win. Meanwhile, the Senators drop the Tigers 4–1 behind Dutch Leonard and the Browns win their first and only pennant. Thanks to Laabs' two long pokes, the jingle about St. Louis ("First in shoes, first in booze and last in the American League") is unsung, if only for this one war-weary year.

1945—Seventeen-year-old Tommy Brown of the Dodgers becomes the youngest player ever to hit a major league home run. Returning from the military in midseason, Hank Greenberg swats a grand slam on the last day of the season to unfurl the flag for the Tigers (see "Short Takes" chapter for details on the Brown homer, "Grandest Slams" for a description of the Greenberg drama).

1950—Philadelphia's "Whiz Kids" nurse a one-game lead down to the last contest of the season. The Dodgers can tie if they win. But Dick Sisler slams a 10th-inning, three-run home run to win the game, 4–1, and a

Red Sox pitcher TRACY STALLARD kicks a little dirt as ROGER MARIS circles the sacks following his record-setting 61st four-bagger in 1961. It was the only run of the game.

pennant for the Phils, the first one in 35 years.

1953—In Washington's Griffith Stadium, Chuck Stobbs serves up an inviting pitch to a muscular young center fielder, Mickey Mantle. Mantle gets all of it and then some. The 565-foot monster home run is the most famous of all tape-measure jobs.

1956—Dale Long of the Pirates hits homers in eight consecutive games.

1961—The Yankees stage the greatest home run circus in history, with Roger Maris individually and the team collectively shattering records, with 61 and 240, respectively. Maris and Mickey Mantle flex their muscles in the Fun City Center Ring. Indeed, until the waning games of the season, the "M and M boys" perform a thrilling act to see which one, or both, will break the Babe's record. In the end, it is the healthy, but media-pressured Maris who accomplishes the incomparable over the injury-nagged Mantle. The Commissioner of Baseball decrees an asterisk after Maris' feat, because he didn't do it within 154 games, as Ruth had. But the M and M duo forms the greatest 1–2 punch in the game's history, Mantle finishing with 54. Four other Yankees, including part-timer John Blanchard, hit more than 20 homers each. (In the Series, Maris, slumping, and Mantle, injured, relinquish the Center Ring to the other Yankee sluggers, as Berra, Howard, Skowron and Blanchard hit five among them and Maris but one.)

HANK AARON connecting for his 715th career home run (Braves, 1974).
Courtesy Atlanta Braves

1963—Willie Mays' 16th-inning long swat breaks up a classic pitching duel between the Giants' Juan Marichal and 42-year-old Braves' southpaw Warren Spahn. The Giants win 1–0.

1968—Frank Howard of the "new" Senators hits 10 HR in six straight games.

1974—History is courted day-by-day as Henry Aaron enters the season with 713 career home runs, one short of the immortal Ruth's record. He hits one early in the season in Cincinnati; then, on April 8, lofts No. 715 before a hometown Atlanta throng and a national television audience.

1981—It's crowded at the top as four players end the curtailed season in an unprecedented four-way tie for the HR lead in the AL. Bobby Grich, Tony Armas, Eddie Murray and Dwight Evans all finish with 22; Greg Luzinski and Gorman Thomas are only one behind the leaders. Of this group, only Thomas ever led before.

Exhibitionists

The All-Star game, pitting those players chosen as best of the NL against the best in the AL, was started in 1933. There was no game in the war year of 1945. There was an experiment with two star games from 1959 through 1962. There have also been other exhibition games where unusual homers have been hit.

1919—Babe Ruth hits four HR for the Red Sox in a spring exhibition game in his hometown of Baltimore, against the Eastern League Orioles. The young Ruth is best known as a pitcher, having just won two games in the 1918 World Series for the victorious Beantowners. Maybe these were the blows that got him really measuring the ball for the fences and revolutionized the game.

1933—Fittingly enough, a now-aging Ruth whacks a two-run long clout in the first-ever All-Star game as the AL wins, 4–2.

1941—Ted Williams, who will go on to lead the league with a .406 batting average, delivers a dramatic gamer in the All-Star contest in Detroit. It is the bottom of the ninth, two out, two on, with the Nationals leading 5–4. The

*A jubilant TED WILLIAMS is greeted at home by JOE DiMAGGIO (No. 5)
after hitting his great gamer in the 1941 All-Star contest. In the regular
season, Williams batted .406 and Joltin' Joe had a 56-game hitting streak.*

Thumper thumps the ball out and the Americans are 7–5 winners. Arky Vaughan hits two long clouts for the NL, a record.

1946—In the days when the AL was still winning some of these things, Ted Williams pokes two out of the park (matching Vaughan's '41 feat) before a hometown crowd in Boston. The Juniors whip the Seniors 12–0. Williams' second is off Rip Sewell's notorious and supposedly unhittable blooper ball, nee eephus pitch.

1950—Ralph Kiner's homer for the NL in the top of the ninth ties the game and leads to the first extra-inning contest in All-Star history. Red Schoendienst puts one away in the 14th to make the Nationals 4–3 winners.

1955—Stan the Man Musial smotes a homer in the bottom of the 12th, sending the Nationals back to regular season play with a 6–5 win.

1960—Musial, pinch-hitting, knocks a HR in the National's 6–0 whitewash. It is his sixth in All-Star competition, the record.

1964—The NL trails the American Stars, 4–3 coming into the bottom of the ninth. Willie Mays gets on and, with some fancy footwork, scores to tie it. The Nationals put two more runners on, then Johnny Callison kisses one goodbye to make the senior circuit 7–4 winners.

1967—The long ball and the long-ball hitter's nemesis, the strikeout, are the story of the All-Star game. By now the National League is winning these mid-season extravaganzas year after year. The longest such game in history goes 15 innings with third basemen Brooks Robinson (AL) and Richie Allen (NL) homers plating the only runs between a lot of fanning the air (30 SO in all). Another third baseman, NLer Tony Perez, knocks the third long shot of the contest into the seats in the top of the 15th and the game ends 2–1 in favor of the Nationals.

1971—Again, home runs account for all the runs, but this time the score is 6–4 in favor of the AL. Reggie Jackson's towering shot over the roof in Detroit is an awesome sight to behold. Even Reggie drops his bat and watches it go. Frank Robinson and Harmon Killebrew also pole two-run home runs for the AL. The National Leaguers likewise bop three (by Johnny Bench, Hank Aaron and Roberto Clemente), but the latter two come with no one on base. It is the American Stars' only victory in 20 consecutive games, from 1963 through 1982.

1982—Seventy-five-year-old Luke Appling hits a home run off 61-year-old Warren Spahn in an old timers game, gaining him a greater volume of fan mail than he ever received as an active player and the lasting admiration of baseball fans of all ages.

1983—In mid-season, the AL breaks its 20-year slump in a big way in the 50th anniversary All-Star game, scoring a record 13 runs to the National's 3. Fred Lynn paces the rout, ramming out the first All-Star grand slam ever during a record-setting seven-run third inning.

The Most

For my money, there are easy winners for the most dramatic, decisive and memorable HR in the four preceding categories. Ranked in order, they are:

Playoffs	1951—Bobby Thomson, Giants
World Series	1960—Bill Mazeroski, Pirates
Regular Season	1938—Gabby Hartnett, Cubs
All-Star Games	1941—Ted Williams, Red Sox

These rankings are consistent with a poll conducted by the Society for American Baseball Research in 1976 to determine the greatest games of all time. The poll of the SABR membership rated the Giants-Dodgers '51 playoff game "the greatest." Ten of the top 21 "all-time" games selected had a HR (or home runs) at center stage. All are mentioned in the preceding pages ('51 Giants-Dodgers playoff game, '60 Pirates-Yankees seventh World Series game, '75 Red Sox-Reds sixth Series game, '20 Indians-Dodgers fifth Series game, '38 Cubs-Pirates game, '41 all-star game, '63 Giants-Braves game, '48 Indians-Red Sox playoff contest, '50 Phillies-Dodgers season-ending game and the '51 Dodgers-Phils season finale).

Ebullient ERNIE BANKS (shown) had some great battles with HANK AARON for the NL home run championship.

George Brace Photo

24

TRYING HARDER

Henry Aaron is sort of the Avis of home runs hitters. He is second to Ruth in the N-ratings and, on three occasions, he was denied a share of the league leadership (and additional N-points) by one blast. Another time he tied for the lead and one time he edged out an opponent by one big blow. However, two other times, he won the title by a wider margin.

In 1957, Aaron edged Ernie Banks, 44–43. But in 1960, in a turnabout-is-fair-play ploy, it was Ernie who won the title over Hank, 41–40. Aaron and Willie McCovey tied for the top in 1963 with 44 each. In 1966–67, it was Hank's turn to edge the opposition; his 44 and 39 long pokes won the league leads by four and two homers, respectively. But Hammerin' Henry had two more near misses, in 1969 and 1971. In '69, it was McCovey 45, Aaron 44 and in '71, Willie Stargell nosed him out, 48–47.

Besides his close races with Aaron in '57 and '60, Banks lost out by a margin of one HR, to Aaron's teammate Eddie Mathews in 1959 (Mathews 46, Banks 45).

Mel Ott also liked to play it close. He won three clear homer titles, beating his closest pursuer by from four to six HR. Three other times, Ott tied for the top and seven times he played bridesmaid, twice losing the title by the margin of one long hit.

Close, But No Cigar . . . Players who missed a tie for the league leadership by one HR.*

American League			National League		
1903	— "Piano Legs" Hickman	12	1913	— Fred Luderus	18
1952	— Luke Easter	31	1914	— Vic Saier	18
1953	— Gus Zernial	41	1916	— Gavvy Cravath	11
1958	— Rocky Colavito	41	1920	— Irish Meusel	14
1960	— Roger Maris	39	1924	— Cy Williams	24
1969	— Frank Howard	48	1929	— Mel Ott	42
1971	— Reggie Jackson	32	1933	— Wally Berger	27
	Norm Cash	32	1934	— Wally Berger	34
1981	— Gorman Thomas	21	1939	— Mel Ott	27
	Greg Luzinski	21	1946	— Johnny Mize	22
			1948	— Stan Musial	39
			1957	— Ernie Banks	43
			1959	— Ernie Banks	45
			1960	— Hank Aaron	40
			1969	— Hank Aaron	44
			1971	— Hank Aaron	47
			1973	— Dave Johnson	43
			1976	— Dave Kingman	37
			1982	— Dale Murphy	36

*Those who missed a share of the title by one HR when the league leader(s) had 10 or less are excluded, because that is at least a 10 percent spread . . . a significant difference.

Note that the AL had no close calls for nearly 50 years, 1903 to 1952. Of the 24 individuals named, 14 did have their place in the sun some other season or seasons, when they won or tied for the top. Those who never basked in the HR limelight: Hickman, Easter, Cash, Luzinski, Luderus, Saier, Meusel, Musial, Johnson and Murphy.

25

OTHER CLAIMS TO FAME

Triple Crowns: Joe (Ducky) Medwick is the only non-BH who has won a triple crown since the Big Hitter era began. Adding in Nap Lajoie and Ty Cobb, triple crown winners from the deadball era, Carl Yastrzemski is the only one to win the triple (league leadership in home runs, runs batted in and batting average) who is not in the Hall of Fame. There's a simple reason why Yaz does not have his name on a plaque in Cooperstown: he's not yet eligible. Ducky and Yaz are also the only ones whose Crowns are slightly tarnished. They tied for the HR lead rather than leading their league outright.

The numbers on the Big Hitters which put the jewels in their crowns in this century:

Year	Player,Team	BH Rank	HR	RBI	BA
1901	Nap Lajoie, Athletics	D-20	14	125	.422
1909	Ty Cobb, Tigers	D14	9	115	.377
1922	Rogers Hornsby, Cardinals	N35	42	152	.401
1925	Rogers Hornsby, Cardinals	N35	39	143	.403
1933	Jimmie Foxx, A's	N5	48	163	.356
1933	Chuck Klein, Phillies	N24 tie	28	120	.368
1934	Lou Gehrig, Yankees	N8	49	165	.363
1937	Joe Medwick, Cardinals	NR**	31*	154	.374
1942	Ted Williams, Red Sox	N 13	36*	137	.356
1947	Ted Williams, Red Sox	N 13	32	114	.343
1956	Mickey Mantle, Yankees	N 6	52	130	.353
1966	Frank Robinson, Orioles	N 11	49	122	.316
1967	Carl Yastrzemski, Red Sox	N 29	44*	121	.326

* Tied for league lead
** Not Ranked

MVP's.

All of the triple crown winners of the Big Hitter era (beginning in 1920) have also won League or Most Valuable Player awards, though not necessarily in the same year they won the triple crown.

Matching TC-MVP performers are Hornsby ('25), Foxx ('33), Medwick ('37), Mantle ('56), Robinson ('66) and Yastrzemski ('67). Those who won the League or MVP honor in years other than their Triple Crown years are Gehrig ('27 and '36), Hornsby ('29), Klein ('32), Foxx ('32 and '38), Williams ('46 and '49), Mantle ('57 and '62) and Robinson ('61).

One in four MVP awardees has been a BH. Counting multiple awards to such sluggers as Stan Musial, Roy Campanella, Jimmie Foxx, Joe DiMaggio and Mickey Mantle (three MVP each) and seven others with two each, more than 40 percent of all Most Valuables have been bestowed on BH in the top 54 so rated.

The MVP award was inaugurated in 1931. Sporadically, other "most valuable" awards were made, the Chalmers award in both leagues, 1911–14 and League Awards in the AL 1922–28 and in the NL 1924-29. BH who won those awards included Cobb, Ruth, Hornsby and Gehrig. It's interesting that Gehrig won the honor in 1927, the year the Bambino touched off 60 HR.

Rookies of the Year

Nine Big Hitters showed early promise of their greatness by being selected Rookie of the Year. Eight of them were National Leaguers, so it appears that it's hard to tell who will develop into a Big Hitter in the AL, based on rookie performance. Only one eventual BH, Roy Sievers, won RY in the American League and he took it in 1949, the first year such awards were made in each league.

However, three of the NL awardees later performed some of their greatest long-ball exploits in the Junior Circuit, Frank Robinson (RY '56), Frank Howard ('60) and Dick Allen ('64). Other Rookie of the Year winners not yet mentioned are Willie Mays ('51), Orlando Cepeda ('58), Willie McCovey ('59), Billy Williams ('61) and Johnny Bench ('68).

Batting Average.

Until recently, BH generally hit for average as well as distance. Fifteen of the top 54 are lifetime .300 hitters. Nowadays, the two dimensions don't seem to mesh too well. Only one active player, Jim Rice, is averaging over .300 (.305, seventh highest among active players). Two active swingers, Dave Kingman and Gorman Thomas, aren't even hitting .250.

The top BH for average are Hornsby (second to Cobb on the lifetime list at .358), Ted Williams (eighth at .344) and Ruth (12th, .342). Lowest are Thomas, .235; Kingman, .237 and Killebrew, .256. The average BA for the 54 leading BH is .284. Perhaps Killebrew's relatively low BA is what is causing Hall of Fame electors to shun him.

26

TRIVIA TIME

Following are tremendous trifles about the top 54 Big Hitters listed in Chapter 2.

Vas You Ever in Spavinaw?

Big Hitters have made it to the big time from all over the country and outside it too. Big Hitters were born in the famous cities like New York, Pittsburgh and Philly, Dallas and Los Angeles.

Some started out in not-so-famous spots. I find these combinations interesting:

• One syllable players from three-syllable towns: Foxx and Cash from Sudlersville and Justiceberg (Maryland and Texas).

• Two K's, Killebrew and Kingman, from two P's: Payette and Pendleton (Idaho and Oregon).

• Two W's from two W's: Cy Williams and Billy Williams from Wadena and Whistler (Indiana and Alabama).

• Lest you think the Midwest is underrepresented, catch this: Two Big Hitters first saw the light of day in Argo and Fargo (but not Chicargo [joke]). Those rhyming towns in Illinois and North Dakota were the birthplaces of Kluszewski and Maris.

Three BH list New York City as their birthplace; Colavito, Gehrig and Greenberg. That's not so surprising. But it is a little unusual that two pairs were born in Mobile, Alabama (Aaron and McCovey) and Beaumont, Texas (Robinson and Zernial).

That Pennsylvania, Texas, California and New York are top producers of top sluggers is not remarkable, either, given their large populations. But that the leading place-of-birth state is Alabama (seven from there) is a bit unusual.

The two born outside the contiguous 48 states are Orlando Cepeda, Puerto Rico and Tony Perez, Cuba.

Finally (and maybe mercifully), to answer this section heading, if you were ever in Spavinaw, Oklahoma, you were in the town where Mickey Mantle was born.

The Long and the Short of It

Frank Howard, 6-foot 7-inches tall and weighing 265 pounds, is the biggest Big Hitter. The next tallest is Dave Kingman (6'6") and the next heaviest Boog Powell (240 pounds).

Mel Ott is the smallest BH (5'9", 170). Shortest is Hack Wilson, 5'6".

Different sources give different heights and weights for the same player, but by an averaging method, I figure the typical BH stands 6'1" and weighs 198.

Both Sides Now

Most of the muscular men (33) swing from the right side of the plate. One, Mantle, was a switch hitter. Nine times in his career, the Mick hit one homer from the right side and one from the left in a single game. Another time, he hit one right-handed and *two* left-handed in the same game.

Big Hits/Good Gloves

It's often said that you can shake the bushes and a dozen gloves will fall out. But the big bats are hard to find. The combination of good glove and big hit is not so common. Only one BH played the toughest fielding position, shortstop. And he (Ernie Banks) played fewer games there than at his "mature" position, first base. But he did hit more than half of his homers while playing short.

The favorite position to station a Big Hitter (and hide his glove?) is first base. Seventeen played the majority of their games at the out-bag. Thirty patrolled the three outfield positions, with 11 known primarily as center fielders, 10 as left fielders and 9 as right fielders. There were some great outfielders among BH, notably center fielders. DiMaggio and Mays were perhaps the best.

Let's see, that then leaves seven Big Hitters for the other three fielding positions, 2B, 3B and C. Rogers Hornsby was the only second sacker. Mathews, Rosen, Santo and Schmidt presided at the hot corner the majority of the time and Bench and Campanella are the catchers.

Three BH (Lee May, Jim Rice and Carl Yastrzemski) have logged quite a few games as designated hitters, but they have been in more games at other positions. At the end of the 1982 season, Jim Rice, Rico Carty and Andre Thornton were tied for most four-baggers hit in a season by a DH, 31 each. Hal McRae has hit more homers as a DH than any other player, 136; McRae leads in almost every other career DH record as well. Don Baylor is the only other player to hit more than 100 career home runs as a designated hitter. Through 1982, he had 121.

A Place to Play

Fifteen of the players listed played all their major league games with one team. (This could change for some of the active players.) Three were Yankees— Gehrig, DiMaggio and Mantle. Yastrzemski has played all 23 years in a Red Sox uniform, one more than Stan Musial did for the Cardinals and Mel Ott for the Giants. At the other end of the spectrum, Bobby Bonds donned eight different uniforms and Dave Kingman has been fitted for six (including four in one year). Rocky Colavito and Richie Allen also appeared on six different teams.

More than half of the performers listed, 29, played exclusively in one league, 15 in the National and 14 in the American. This could also change for the actives.

Thirty-one played all or the majority of games in the NL, 22 in the AL. Frank Robinson divided his time and talent about equally between the two leagues. The evidence is that he was named the Most Valuable Player twice, once in each league and that he hit for the distance in 32 different major league parks in his long career.

The Lineup

My all-Big Hitter lineup would have Jimmie Foxx (N-5) catching, Lou Gehrig (N-8) at first base, Rogers Hornsby (N-36) at second base, Ernie Banks (N-10) at shortstop, Eddie Mathews (N-9) at third base, Hank Aaron (N-2) in left field, Willie Mays (N-3) in center field, Babe Ruth (N-1) in right field and Wes Ferrell pitching (National League rules) or Harmon Killebrew (N-4) as designated hitter. Mickey Mantle (N-6), a switch-hitter, could come in in any situation to pinch hit and the first man off the bench would be Bench (Johnny, that is, N-26 tie). Bench could handle the catching chores or fill in at first, third or in the outfield. Sadly, this all-bruiser lineup would have no good spot for Ralph Kiner (N-7).

Hornsby would probably have to lead off and Banks would bat eighth or ninth in the order. If these starters (under the DH rule) would hit about their average number of home runs, my team would sock 247. That's only seven more than the 1961 Yankees actually did clout and they did it without benefit of the DH. It demonstrates what a large role longevity plays in piling up N-points.

However, if the players on this all-slugging team (again under the DH) all simultaneously had their *best* year, they would send 451 out, an average of 50 per man.

The single-season records for home runs by each position, counting only wallops while the player was actually playing that position:

Catcher—Roy Campanella, Dodgers, 41, '53

First Baseman—Hank Greenberg, 58, Tigers, '38

Second Baseman—Rogers Hornsby, Cardinals, '22 and Dave Johnson, Braves, '73, both 42

Third Baseman—Mike Schmidt, Phils, 48, '80

Shortstop—Ernie Banks, Cubs, 47, '58

Left Field—Ralph Kiner, Pirates, 54, '49

Center Field—Hack Wilson, Cubs, 56, '30

Right Field—Roger Maris, Yanks, 61, '61

Pitcher—Wes Ferrell, Indians, 9, '31

Designated Hitter—Jim Rice, Red Sox, '77, Rico Carty, A's, '78 and Andre Thornton, Indians, '82, each 31

This team, with a DH, would hit 438 homers, an average of about 49 per man.

The Consummate Ballplayer

Considering all of the foregoing, it is possible to construct a composite Big Hitter. He is 6-feet-1 inch and 198 pounds. He plays first base and bats right-handed. He is a National Leaguer and hails from, strangely enough, New York City, Alabama. That makes Johnny Bench the typical Big Hitter on days he's playing first base, except he's from Oklahoma.

27

LEGENDS IN LEFT FIELD

When 42-year-old Ted Williams trotted from his left field position for the final time in 1960, everyone knew he left a legend there. When a youngster half his age named Carl Yastrzemski assumed the same spot in front of the "green monster" in Boston's Fenway Park the following spring, could Red Sox fans know a second legend had taken up residence in left field?

The successive legends spanned 45 years, from 1939 through 1983 (after which "Yaz" hung 'em up). To call Williams and Yastrzemski back-to-back legends with their backs against that close-in, high-standing fence is somewhat generic. Williams began his career as a right fielder. Yaz, as nearly everyone eventually shortened his long last name, finished up as a designated hitter. But both, by far, played most of their games in left.

That the legendary athletes played the same positions on the same team one after the other is interesting. That their characteristics and accomplishments are similar adds more interest.

Carl was born in the same year (1939) that Ted launched his major league career. Their birthdays are only a few days apart, August 22 (Yaz) and August 30 (Williams).

The Williams legend extended through 22 years. The Yastrzemski legend reached 23. Ted hit 521 home runs, tied for eighth on the career list and good for 14th in the N-ratings. Yaz had lofted 442 through the 1982 season for No. 17 career and No. 28 (tie) "N."

Though in defense they both had to watch balls going over or off the great wall for opposition home runs and other hits, they were denied a good chance to reciprocate at bat, because both were left-handed batters. Left-

and right-handed batters face quite different challenges at Fenway. The barrier looms only about 350 feet away in the left-center power alley, but 37 feet high. Right-center lies more than 380 feet distant and is bounded by a low fence. A high pop fly will clear the Monster near the line (315 feet); it takes a long, hard poke to reach the seats any place in right except right near the foul pole.

So their home playing field thrust difficult homer-hitting assignments upon both of them (this was especially true for Ted, a dead pull hitter for whom the "Williams shift"—three infielders to the right of second base— was originated).

Both Williams and Yaz had a "good eye." In baseball lingo, a good eye doesn't necessarily mean the batter possesses extraordinary eyesight, although Williams is often credited with having about as keen vision as is humanly possible. A good eye usually means a batter can pick out good pitches to hit and lay off the bad ones. Regardless of the degree of physical visual acuity, they both definitely had a good eye. Yaz ranks first in average walks per home run among the top Big Hitters (about 4 BB per HR) and Williams comes home second (about 3.9). Of course, factors like intentional walks and "pitching around" a hitter go into this statistic and have little to do with selectivity. But the good eye is the main reason for a high ratio.

Here are the lengends' all-time "top 20" rankings in important hitting measures, together with their single-season best performances in each category through 1982:

	Career				Single Season Highs			
	Williams		**Yastrzemski**		**Williams**		**Yastrzemski**	
	Measure/Rank		**Measure/Rank**		**Measure/Year**		**Measure/Year**	
Games	2292	NR***	3189	2	156	'47	162	'69
At Bats	7706	NR	11608	3	566	'49	646	'62
Hits	2654	NR	3318	7	194	'49	191	'62
Doubles	525	18	622	8	44	'41&'48*	45*	'65
Triples	71	NR	59	NR	14	'40	9	'64
Home Runs	521	8tie	442	17	43*	'49	44**	'67
HR %	6.8	6	3.8	NR	9.0*	'57	7.6	'67
Runs	1798	12	1778	13	150	'49	125	'70
RBI	1839	10	1788	13	159*	'49	121*	'67
Walks	2019	2	1790	3	162*	'47&'49	128	'70
Strikeouts	709	NR	1364	20	64	'39	96	'61
Stolen Bases	24	NR	170	NR	4	'40&'48	23	'70
Batting	.344	8	.286	NR	.406*	'41	.329	'70
Slugging	.634	2	.464	NR	.735*	'41	.622*	'67

   * — League Lead
  ** — Tied for League Lead
*** — Not Ranked in the "Top 20"

Note how close Yaz' runs, runs-batted-in and bases-on-balls figures are, both for career and season bests. Williams' season bests were strung out over 17 years ('41–'57); Yastrzemski packed his into nine ('62–'70). (Strikeouts are not "bests.")

Ted wasn't much of a threat to steal, averaging about one a year. In six different full seasons, he didn't swipe one. But was he tough to fan!

When Carl gets in 110 games in '83 he will displace Henry Aaron as the all-time leader in games played. If he scores 20 or more runs (looks easy), he will move ahead of Ted in that category and can also pass him in RBI (52 needed).

Williams is in the Baseball Hall of Fame. Yastrzemski will be there. Williams won the Triple Crown (BA, HR, RBI) in '42 and '47; Yaz did it in '67. Yastrzemski was named Most Valuable Player in the AL in the same year, '67. The Splendid Splinter took the honors twice, but in different years from his Triple Crowns ('46 and '49).

Yastrzemski's greatest year was without doubt 1967. Williams had great numbers three times, '42, '47 and '49, with '49 his best power year. A case could be made for '41, too (nobody has batted .400 since).

It is important to remember in comparing the performances of these two living legends that Williams' career extended over 22 years, but he missed all or most of five seasons due to military service in World War II and the Korean conflict. He was an eagle-eyed pilot. Yaz was "always there." He has appeared in the majority of Bosox games every year he's played.

Yaz, who turned 44 during the '83 championship season, wrested the over-40 HR title from Williams (see "Life Begins at 40" chapter).

Last time I looked, Fenway Park's left fielder was Jim Rice, a great player in his own right. Like Yaz and Ted before him, he broke in the year he turned age 21. With nine years behind him through 1982, he's got about 13 left to write HIS legend.

28

A TALE OF TWO SLUGGERS: ROGER MARIS AND HACK WILSON *

The year 1980 was the Golden Anniversary of Hack Wilson's great power season. The 25th anniversary of Roger Maris' great year will come before the end of the decade.

If you were asked what Wilson and Maris had in common, your reply might be: "Wilson holds the record for home runs in the National League, Maris has the American League Record." That would be correct.

But are there other things? You might also say: "Roger holds a significant *major* league record, for home runs in a season, and Hack set one too, for runs-batted-in."

---

*Expanded from an article by the same name and author in *The National Pastime*, Vol. 1, No. 1, 1982, pp.32-33.

ROGER MARIS watches No. 61 go (Yankees, 1961).

HACK WILSON holds the National League single-season home run record.

George Brace Photo

Fine. Anything else? "Well," you might go on, "each had his troubles after his big year (1930 for Cub Wilson and 1961 for Yank Maris), never getting anywhere near their great year again and each retiring at a relatively young age." You might also add, "and both were outfielders."

These are similarities enough. But they are only the beginning of a long list of "likes" that gets to be positively weird if we dig deep enough into the careers of both men.

Try these striking comparisons:

Both players started their careers slowly, made a meteoric dash to fame and then took a fast slide to retirement. Both spent 12 years in the major leagues.

Both were rookies in their 23rd year; Wilson played his last major league games in 1934 at age *34*; *34* years later, in 1968, Maris played his last season, also at age 34.

Each had his second-best home run output the year before his big campaign and each hit exactly 39 home runs in those years.

Similarities enough? No. We're just warming up. When Maris clouted his 61, teammate Mickey Mantle also had his greatest home run season, hitting 54. Wilson also had a teammate enjoying his greatest long ball year. Gabby Hartnett connected for a career high 37 round-trippers the same year Wilson lifted 56.

The Maris-Mantle total of 115 HR's is the American and Major League season record for two players on the same club. Wilson and Hartnett's 93 are the most ever hit by two National League teammates in a season.

They are close in the N-ratings. Wilson has 114 N-points (a tie for 28th in the rankings), Maris 97 (tie for 36th).

I mentioned Wilson's major league record of 190 runs-batted-in in 1930. Hack led the league that year and also the year before, when he drove 159 across. Maris also led the league in the year before THE year and topped that with 142 to lead the league and set a personal high in 1961. Neither ever led the league in RBIs in any other year.

Not surprisingly, Maris and Wilson set several other personal highs in their record-shattering years. Besides home runs and RBIs, Wilson had the highest batting average and most games played, at-bats, runs, HR percentage, bases on balls, slugging average and hits for him ever. Maris (naturally) also had personal highs in games, at bats, runs, HR percentage, BB, slugging average and hits, though he did match his at bat total the next season. Maris tied for the league lead in runs, in addition to his HR and RBI titles. Wilson also had league leaderships besides HRs and RBIs in 1930 (HR percentage, BB, slugging average), but two others weren't the most coveted achievements; Hack led the National League in striking out and outfielders in errors.

Both were about the same threat to poke it out of the park: Hack's career homers-to-at-bats ratio was 1 to 19.5; Roger's rate was 1 homer for every 18.5 official plate appearances. They had about the same totals for walks (Wilson 674, Maris 652) and strikeouts (Maris 733, Wilson 713).

Both started and closed their careers with teams other than those with which they achieved stardom. Maris was with the Indians and A's before putting on the Yankee pinstripes. He was traded to the Cardinals for his last two professional years. Wilson began as a Giant, closed out with the Dodgers and Phillies (he spent a year in the minors before he called it quits).

Each played for pennant winners other than his principal team, Maris on the '67 and '68 Cards and Wilson on the '24 Giants.

At this point, you may be saying "Hold on a minute. You can find these kinds of similarities between many ballplayers. For example, Babe Ruth also started and finished with teams other than his starring team (Red Sox to start, Braves to finish). He likewise played on other Series teams, the Red Sox of 1915, '16 and '18 as a pitcher. And he was later and greater an outfielder by trade."

True enough, but not striking enough. It's hard to find other similarities after these points are passed. By contrast, we're still not through in comparing the almost eerie similarities in the careers of these two, shall we say, star-crossed swingers, Hack Wilson and Roger Maris, who performed great batting feats a generation apart.

As I noted at the outset, neither Wilson nor Maris again achieved anywhere near the heights of their big seasons after the big year. Wilson's best power year following his tremendous 1930 campaign of 56 homers and 190 RBI was when he hit a mere 23 and drove in 123 runs two years later, batting a subpar, for him, .297. Maris' best was the year following his record-setter, when he managed 33 round-trippers, drove in 100 runs and batted .256. (Ruth still had many great years left in his big bat after *his* big year.)

Perhaps most puzzling about the careers of both men is that their historic feats have failed to win them lasting admiration, even among their own fans. Maris couldn't qualify on the all-time Yankee team which fans picked in 1969. Of course, it would be hard for anybody to dislodge any member of the Yankee dream outfield of Ruth, Mantle and Joe DiMaggio.

Wilson's achievement of 56 homers, though a National League record that has endured for more than 50 years, couldn't have been too thrilling at the time, coming so soon after Ruth had blasted 60 (and also 59 and 54 twice) so recently. Besides, he did it at a time when an exhausted nation was plummeting into the Great Depression. Also, Hack was playing for a second-place team. Wilson also came off as somewhat of a heavy. He was no glamour-boy, appearance-wise, and had problems with the booze.

Maris was considered by some to be more of a villain than a hero for his 1961 triumphs. Many pointed out that Rog had the benefit of a 162-game schedule and expansion teams to face in cracking Ruth's mark. And, to add insult to injury, he had the audacity to overshadow the long-ball feats of another latter-day Yankee favorite, Mantle, at the same time he was violating the immortal Ruth's 60-homer record. And the nation was again on the brink of agonizing years, Vietnam, unrest, violence in the streets.

It remains to be seen if Maris will ever have his name enshrined in the Hall of Fame. Wilson's name waited for more than three decades to be elevated to that place of high honor in Cooperstown.

I must honestly add that these two ill-fated athletes did not have *everything* about them and their careers in such fascinating parallel.

Wilson hit for a higher career average (.307) than Maris (.260). Maris never batted .300 in the majors, .283 in 1960 was his best. Wilson topped the magic .300 mark five times; his best year was his big year, 1930, when he averaged .356. However, their batting averages are not too much different, considering the eras when they performed. During Wilson's career, the average National Leaguer batted .283. In Maris' time, the average ballplayer batted 33 points less (.250).

Maris was the AL home run champion in only that one year, 1961. Wilson won or tied for the NL top three other times (in 1926, '27 and '28). Maris had three 100-RBI years, Wilson six, but in an era when big RBI seasons were more common than in Maris' time. Maris played in seven World Series in all—five with the Yankees and two with the Cardinals. Wilson was in just two. Maris hit for power in the fall classic (six home runs), but not for average (.217). Wilson hit for average in series games (.319), but did not hit a single home run (in 47 at bats).

Physically, Maris was a nicely proportioned 6 feet by 200 pounds. Wilson on the other hand was a real shorty, packing 190 pounds on a squat 5-foot-six frame. Maris was left-handed all the way; Wilson threw righty and batted from the right side; Maris was a Northerner (born in North Dakota), Wilson from the East (Pennsylvania). They starred in different leagues at different times and played on no teams in common.

But it still seems almost supernatural when you continue to compare the two. Ready for some more?

Wilson had more home runs in his one great year than in the first four major league seasons he played or the last four combined; the Pennsylvania Pounder hit more than half of his career homers in the three consecutive seasons of 1928 through 1930. Maris' home run career fits the same mold: The Dakota Strong Boy had more round trippers in 1961 than in his first three seasons put together or in his last four; he also hit almost half of his career home runs in three consecutive campaigns—1960 through 1962.

Wilson closed out his career with only 15 four-baggers in his last two seasons (9 and 6) and, true to form, Maris followed suit almost exactly, with 14 (9 and 5).

And then there was . . . What? "Stop!" did you say? "Hold it! That's enough!" Maybe that is enough. But let's just look at this one other striking similarity:

In their respective final seasons,each had virtually identical pinch-hitting records (Wilson 5 hits in 20 at-bats, Maris 6 for 21).

This, then is "A Tale of Two Sluggers:" Hack Wilson and Roger Maris. It's a little spooky to me.

Hack Wilson, OF (Lewis Robert) b. April 26, 1900			Roger Maris, OF (Roger Eugene) b. September 10, 1934		
		Home			Home
Year	Team	Runs	RBI	Year	Team	Runs	RBI

Year	Team	Home Runs	RBI	Year	Team	Home Runs	RBI
1923	Giants	0	0	1957	Indians	1 4	51
1924	Giants	10	57	1958	Ind's-A's	28	80
1925	Giants	6	30	1959	A's	16	72
1926	Cubs	21x	109	1960	Yankees	39	112x
1927	Cubs	30xx	129	1961	Yankees	61x*	142x
1928	Cubs	31xx	120	1962	Yankees	33	100
1929	Cubs	39	159x	1963	Yankees	23	53
1930	Cubs	56x**	190x*	1964	Yankees	26	71
1931	Cubs	13	61	1965	Yankees	8	27
1932	Dodgers	23	123	1966	Yankees	13	43
1933	Dodgers	9	54	1967	Cardinals	9	55
1934	Dodgers-Phils	6	30	1968	Cardinals	5	45
2 years-4 teams		244	1062	12 years-4 teams		275	851

x — League Lead
xx — Tie for Lead
* — Major League Record
** — National League Record

BABE RUTH, the would-be king, greeted by LOU GEHRIG following the Bambino's 60th home run (Yankees, 1927).

29

THE WOULD-BE KING

Little Willie Keeler used to "hit 'em where they ain't." He twice had 200 or more singles in a season, the only player to ever accomplish that (202 in 1898 and 200 in '97). That was fine for Willie's day and his wee kind.

Along about 1919–20, though, some baseball players began to discover they didn't have the speed, agility and ability to consistently hit 'em where they ain't; within the confines of the ball park, that is. So, if they were strong enough, they started going for the bleachers where there ain't no fielders either. Nearer fences, (possibly) livelier balls, more frequent ball changes, outlawing of some trick pitches and other circumstances helped the long-ball boys.

Thus the finesse game began to wane and the power game began to come into prominence. Babe Ruth, all 6-foot-2 inches and (at least) 215 pounds of him, a large man for those days, was the leader of the pack which started the new pounding game. The fans loved it and they loved Ruth most of all.

Babe Ruth/home run; the name and the term are inseparable. They belong together like peaches/cream; like thunder/lightning; like Abe Lincoln/great president.

Emerging from World War I, America was beginning to feel its collective muscle. Ruth was muscle personified, in deed if not exactly in appearance. America, especially its young males, began to make of Ruth a national hero. One only need scan the long list of his heroic accomplishments to pretty quickly arrive at the conclusion that there are heroes and then there are Heroes. In Ruth's case, with the image of a whole burgeoning Nation to represent, it was just as quickly apparent that *he* was a capital "H" hero. But Hero was not quite enough for some.

The Nation continued its growth and more and more admired its own swelling muscle. Ruth, too, kept on becoming more Heroic, 29 homers for the record, then 54, eventually 60, with three 40-plus years salted in.

First to hit 200 home runs. And 300, 400, 500, 600 and 700. First to hit three homers in one World Series game. First to knock a round-tripper in an All-Star game. First to send a baseball completely out of several ball parks. First to draw such-and-such a salary and such-and-such a crowd. First to predict precisely when and where he would hit one out (disputed and doubted, but mostly believed). The record for eating hot dogs with mustard in one sitting (not too carefully documented). First after first. Record after record. A walking, talking, performing record book, a new edition ever day.

I doubt it was ever spoken and probably was not even whispered, but it must have flitted through many a man's and boy's mind: "Let's crown him King." After all, he had become the best-known American on the face of the Earth.

I for one have a certain amount of envy of our British brothers. They have always had a royal family, a king or queen and a court to be adored and gossiped about. Ah, but there's the rub. The Declaration of Independence, that most venerated of American documents, tells us in no uncertain terms that we must not have a king. We created a new country precisely to get away from a tyrannical king.

It's all there, right up front in unmistakeable terms: "Governments are instituted among Men, deriving their just Powers from the Consent of the Governed . . ." But wait a minute: If the governed consent to a king, why not crown one?

We must read further into that great document of 1776 to find out why not: ". . . The History of the present King of Great Britain is a History of repeated Injuries and Usurpations . . ." Oh.

But if we can derive our "just Powers . . ." Hold on there, we were talking about kings. Let the Declaration of Independence tell us some more about kings, or at least this one specific king. The John Hancock-signed parchment continues with a long list (capitalized or not capitalized as put down by its authors) of refusals, forbiddances, dissolutions, preventions, obstructions, harassments, subjections, pretensions, mockeries, impositions, deprivations, Punishments, Offenses, abolitions, arbitrarianisms, suspensions, abdications, constrainments, Oppressions, Insurrections and Injuries, all perpetrated in a merciless and Murderous manner. Pretty strong stuff. To cap it off, ". . . A Prince whose Character is thus marked by every act which may define a Tyrant, is unfit to be the Ruler of a free People." So there.

Still, the minds of more modern man must have continued to reason: "Well, 1776 was a long time ago (even in the '20s). Babe Ruth wouldn't do any of these terrible things to us. He was certainly not to the manor born. He's such a lovable guy. We are going to thrust this crown upon him; he is not taking it by divine right."

Maybe so. But our founding fathers were just and wise and stern men, saying, implicitly, "What happened with one king could happen with another. We told you no more kings and we meant it."

Yankee ingenuity to the fore again. What was hit upon in the minds of the adoring throng was a neat compromise, an amalgam which would satisfy the lust for a king, but present the outward appearance of only a hero, thus escaping the terrible wrath of the founding fathers. The trick was to make the Sultan of Swat a Hero/king (big H, little k).

Ruth was perfect for the role. He held court but did not permit himself to be courted (as in tirelessly visiting hospitals and prisons and autographing ball after bat after scorecard). He let the people fashion a crown and a robe and a throne, but he never actually put on the trappings and he never sat on the exalted seat. He gathered the acclaim by action and deed, not by some sort of divine right. He earned his heroism and accepted the resultant kingly worship.

Baseball was the national pastime, the American game, the king of sports. And Ruth ruled baseball.

If you're snickering a bit about all of this, think about something else: The American system would suggest that if anybody could come close to being a king, it would have to be the president, the top man in the government instituted among men. But presidents can be pretty poorly suited for the role. They tend to be stodgy lawyers or distant generals or just plain politicians, who may never do anything particularly heroic or even exciting.

Ruth proved, to his subjects' delight, that presidents are pretty ordinary, unheroic folks. He (allegedly) was introduced to President Calvin Coolidge before a ball game one sweltering day, and commented: "Hot as hell, ain't it Prez?" His most famous quotation, again perhaps apocryphal, was in answer to a question of why he, Babe Ruth, ball-player, should draw a larger salary ($80,000) than Herbert Hoover, President ($75,000). His reply: "I had a better year than he did."

Whatever you think of this entire Ruthian rumination (I had to get it out of my system somehow), whether you think he was Hero/king or merely

Yankee/right fielder, this much to me is for sure: What Ruth sowed and reaped was the greatest harvest in sports history and maybe American history. And he did it in a simple, straightforward, Lincolnesque way that delighted the American culture. He simply hit Heroic home runs like nobody before or since.

30

AFTERWORD: 1983

Because of publishing deadlines, it was not possible to completely update this book through 1983. Following are some highlights of the '83 campaign, however.

Regular Season

Mike Schmidt's big year (40 home runs, most in the majors) vaulted him into ninth place in the N-ratings, ahead of Eddie Mathews. Ernie Banks dropped from the top 10. Another big year for Mike could propel him past Gehrig, Kiner and Mantle into the No. 6 spot, just behind Jimmie Foxx.

Jim Rice led the American league with 39 big blasts. That performance allowed him to move from 43rd to 31st, quite a jump. Jim Rice and Cecil Cooper tied for the league leadership in RBI. Each had 126. The other slugger who made great strides in the upper reaches of the ratings was Greg Luzinski, who hit 32 homers to move from 63rd to a tie for the No. 50 spot.

For the second straight year, Dale Murphy finished second in home runs in the National League. However, off that performance, he is now one of the top 100 Big Hitters. Murphy also joined the select "30–30 club," one of only six players who has swatted 30 or more homers and swiped 30 or more bases in the same season (he had 36 and 30, respectively). Murphy led the league in RBI with 121.

Tony Armas finished second to Rice in the American with 36 home runs. That marked the first time since 1961 that AL teammates have finished one-two in the home run derby. Both Rice and Armas play for the Red Sox.

***MIKE SCHMIDT'S** big year vaulted him into the ninth spot in the N-ratings (Phillies, 1983).*

The White Sox found the power the South Siders have so often lacked in the past, with rookie Ron Kittle cracking 35 round-trippers and designated hitter Luzinski catching up to 32 pitches and belting them out. That was a new record for HR by a DH.

Schmidt, Kittle and Luzinski helped their teams to divisional titles and Murphy's clubbing kept the Braves close. The Red Sox, who also had the league batting champion (Wade Boggs), found no magic in the home run, however, as they wound up sixth in the AL East Division.

It was a little sad in Boston for another reason. Carl Yastrzemski called it a career. And what a career it was. During 1983, he played in his 3,308th game, surpassing Hank Aaron for the honor and tied a record for most seasons with one club, 23. He also set standards for four-baggers by a player 40 years old or older and stands alone for knockin' em out in the year he reached age 44 (10 home runs in '83). Yaz wrote the last line in his legend when he played left field in Fenway in the final game of the year. It had been more than three years since he took up his position in front of the Green Monster. Yaz did not bow out so gloriously as Ted Williams had in 1960, when he homered in his last time up. Yastrzemski popped up. But Yaz did surpass his illustrious predecessor in two career categories, runs scored and RBI.

The other BH to slip into retirement was Johnny Bench. Much younger than Yaz, his many years of crouching behind the plate took its toll and he did not have a chance to "taper off" in a DH role as Yatrzemski did. He too played his entire major league career for one team, the Reds.

George Foster's 28 long wallops moved him up two places in the N-ratings. Two other Big Hitters, Reggie Jackson and Dave Kingman, had forgettable years. Reggie had 14 home runs and batted .194; Dave's comparative numbers were 13 and .198. Jackson was AL co-champion in home runs in 1982 (39) and Kingman won the '82 NL crown with 37.

Players active in 1983 who now have more than 100 N-points:

	N-Points	Rank
Schmidt	218	9
Jackson	162	17
Bench	118	26
Yastrzemski	115	28
Foster	108	30
Rice	107	31[x]
Kingman	104	34

X—Three-way tie with Musial and Cepeda.

"The Bull," GREG LUZINSKI, *set a new record for home runs in a season by a designated hitter (White Sox, 1983).*

Courtesy Chicago White Sox

A Sticky Situation

The stickiest situation of the season was caused by George Brett's tarred bat. The "Tar Wars" were battled by Brett, the Yankees, umpires and American League President Lee MacPhail. The conflict went something like this:

Brett bopped a top-of-the-ninth homer to put the Royals ahead of the Yankees. The Yanks claimed an illegal weapon was used to do the deed (pine tar too far up the bat). The umpires agreed, disallowed the HR, called Brett out and said the Yankees won the game. Brett and his teammates got mad and protested. MacPhail, saying things about the "spirit" of the game and the faultiness of the rules, reversed the umps, allowed the homer and decreed the game go on at a later date.

Now the Yankees got furious. But there was no appeal on MacPhail's ruling. The game was quietly completed at the "later date," the Royals prevailing. For all the sparring over the tarring, the war was hardly worth the warring. The Royals finished second in the AL West, but 20 games behind the White Sox. Had the Yankees won the war, they would have tied for second in the East, six games behind the Orioles, instead of third a game back of the Tigers.

League Championships

Good pitching dominated the championships in both leagues, with three shutouts, four games in which one team scored one run and three additional instances of a team being held to two scores. But homers provided four of the six game-winning RBI for the champion Phillies and Orioles.

Mike Schmidt's first-inning homer in the first game of the National League playoffs was the only run of the game as the Phils beat the Dodgers. But Gary Matthews was the series batting star as he homered in each of the three remaining games. His second-game big hit was in vain as the Phils lost 4–1. But he paced identical-score 7–2 victories in games three and four with two more long bombs. His third-game hit was a solo job, but his three-run first-inning wallop in the finale was the game winner. Gary drove in eight runs, had five straight hits in one stretch and batted .429 for the series.

There were just three home runs in the Orioles' three-games-to-one triumph over the White Sox in the American League playoffs. All were hit by Bird batters. After the Chisox had gritted out a homerless 2–1 opening game win, Gary Roenicke's two-run shot in the sixth inning of the second contest sewed up a 4–0 shutout. Eddie Murray's three-run clout in the opening frame of game three was all the Baltimore bashers really needed in an 11–1 crusher. A classic scoreless tussle in the final game ended

GEORGE BRETT'S tarred bat led to a sticky situation (Royals, 1983).

abruptly when courageous Sox starter Britt Burns' 150th pitch of the game proved to be one pitch too many. One of the unlikeliest Orioles, Tito Landrum, belted it into the stands in the top of the 10th. The Orioles quickly got two more runners across the plate and completed the shutout in the bottom of the inning. The Chicagoans paid the price for their power failure; they scored but three runs in the four games.

World Series

For the World Champion Orioles, the Series was almost a replay of their league championship. They dropped the first game at home to the Phillies (again by a 2–1 margin), then won the rest. All of the first-game runs scored on three home runs. The O's wound up with six four-baggers in the Series, including three in their convincing 5–0 clincher. The record for round-trippers in a five-game Series was set by the previous Oriole big winner. The 1970 champs socked 10.

Mike Schmidt, the heavy hitter in the majors for regular-season homers and whose blast in the first game of the playoffs got the Phillies rolling, endured a miserable performance at bat in the Series. Mike not only did not homer, he got only one shattered-bat single in the October classic. Eddie Murray, the Orioles' big hit man, was failing his team with even more regularity than Schmidt until the final game. Then steady Eddie uncoiled for two long homers and a single to finish with a flourish.

In the final analysis, it was Baltimore's pitching and their "everybody contributes" team concept that made the Series difference.

31
UNFINISHED BUSINESS

This ends my tale
Of the Big Hit
And the men who hit them,
The Big Hitters.

But the game of baseball
Is an endless story.

So the saga continues
And some of what is writ here
Will be rewritten
Time and again.

As the great games go on
On the green fields of summer.

Under the sweating sun
On growing grass
And beneath the buzzing lights
On plastic mats.

Go for it!

APPENDICES

APPENDIX 1—HOME RUN LEADERS BY YEAR

YEAR	NL Home Run Leader	AL Home Run Leader
1901	Sam Crawford-16	Nap Lajoie-14
1902	Tommy Leach-6	Socks Seybold-16
1903	Jimmie Sheckard-9	Buck Freeman-13
1904	Harry Lumley-9	Harry Davis-10
1905	Fred Odwell-9	Harry Davis-8
1906	Tim Jordan-12	Harry Davis-12
1907	Dave Brain-10	Harry Davis-8
1908	Tim Jordan-12	Sam Crawford-7
1909	Red Murray-7	Ty Cobb-9
1910	Frank Schulte-10	Jake Stahl-10
	Fred Beck-10	
1911	Frank Schulte-21	Frank Baker-11
1912	Heinie Zimmerman-14	Frank Baker-10
		Tris Speaker-10
1913	Gavvy Cravath-19	Frank Baker-12
1914	Gavvy Cravath-19	Frank Baker-9
1915	Gavvy Cravath-24	Braggo Roth-7
1916	Cy Williams-12	Wally Pipp-12
	Dave Robertson-12	

YEAR	NL Home Run Leader	AL Home Run Leader
1917	Gavvy Cravath-12	Wally Pipp-9
	Dave Robertson-12	
1918	Gavvy Cravath-8	Babe Ruth-11
		Tilly Walker-11
1919	Gavvy Cravath-12	Babe Ruth-29
1920	Cy Williams-15	Babe Ruth-54
1921	George Kelly-23	Babe Ruth-59
1922	Rogers Hornsby-42	Ken Williams-39
1923	Cy Williams-41	Babe Ruth-41
1924	Jack Fournier-27	Babe Ruth-46
1925	Rogers Hornsby-39	Bob Meusel-33
1926	Hack Wilson-21	Babe Ruth-47
1927	Cy Williams-30	Babe Ruth-60
	Hack Wilson-30	
1928	Hack Wilson-31	Babe Ruth-54
	Jim Bottomley-31	
1929	Chuck Klein-43	Babe Ruth-46
1930	Hack Wilson-56	Babe Ruth-49
1931	Chuck Klein-31	Babe Ruth-46
		Lou Gehrig-46
1932	Mel Ott-38	Jimmie Foxx-58
	Chuck Klein-38	
1933	Chuck Klein-28	Jimmie Foxx-48
1934	Mel Ott-35	Lou Gehrig-49
	Rip Collins-35	
1935	Wally Berger-34	Jimmie Foxx-36
		Hank Greenberg-36
1936	Mel Ott-33	Lou Gehrig-49
1937	Mel Ott-31	Joe DiMaggio-46
	Joe Medwick-31	
1938	Mel Ott-36	Hank Greenberg-58
1939	Johnny Mize-28	Jimmie Foxx-35
1940	Johnny Mize-43	Hank Greenberg-41
1941	Dolf Camilli-34	Ted Williams-37
1942	Mel Ott-30	Ted Williams-36
1943	Bill Nicholson-29	Rudy York-34
1944	Bill Nicholson-33	Nick Etten-22
1945	Tommy Holmes-28	Vern Stephens-24
1946	Ralph Kiner-23	Hank Greenberg-44

YEAR	NL Home Run Leader	AL Home Run Leader
1947	Ralph Kiner-51	Ted Williams-32
	Johnny Mize-51	
1948	Ralph Kiner-40	Joe DiMaggio-39
	Johnny Mize-40	
1949	Ralph Kiner-54	Ted Williams-43
1950	Ralph Kiner-47	Al Rosen-37
1951	Ralph Kiner-42	Gus Zernial-33
1952	Ralph Kiner-37	Larry Doby-32
	Hank Sauer-37	
1953	Eddie Mathews-47	Al Rosen-43
1954	Ted Kluszewski-49	Larry Doby-32
1955	Willie Mays-51	Mickey Mantle-37
1956	Duke Snider-43	Mickey Mantle-52
1957	Hank Aaron-44	Roy Sievers-42
1958	Ernie Banks-47	Mickey Mantle-42
1959	Eddie Mathews-46	Harmon Killebrew-42
		Rocky Colavito-42
1960	Ernie Banks-41	Mickey Mantle-40
1961	Orlando Cepeda-46	Roger Maris-61
1962	Willie Mays-49	Harmon Killebrew-48
1963	Willie McCovey-44	Harmon Killebrew-45
	Hank Aaron-44	
1964	Willie Mays-47	Harmon Killebrew-49
1965	Willie Mays-52	Tony Conigliaro-32
1966	Hank Aaron-44	Frank Robinson-49
1967	Hank Aaron-39	Harmon Killebrew-44
		Carl Yastrzemski-44
1968	Willie McCovey-36	Frank Howard-44
1969	Willie McCovey-45	Harmon Killebrew-49
1970	Johnny Bench-45	Frank Howard-44
1971	Willie Stargell-48	Bill Melton-33
1972	Johnny Bench-40	Richie Allen-37
1973	Willie Stargell-44	Reggie Jackson-32
1974	Mike Schmidt-36	Richie Allen-32
1975	Mike Schmidt-38	Reggie Jackson-36
		George Scott-36
1976	Mike Schmidt-38	Graig Nettles-32
1977	George Foster-52	Jim Rice-39
1978	George Foster-40	Jim Rice-46
1979	Dave Kingman-48	Gorman Thomas-45

YEAR	NL Home Run Leader	AL Home Run Leader
1980	Mike Schmidt-48	Reggie Jackson-41
		Ben Oglivie-41
1981	Mike Schmidt-31	Bobby Grich-22
		Eddie Murray-22
		Dwight Evans-22
		Tony Armas-22
1982	Dave Kingman-37	Reggie Jackson-39
		Gorman Thomas-39

APPENDIX 2—THE TOP 100 BIG HITTERS
(Through 1982 Season)

KEY: Career HR/Rank—No. Homers in career/Rank among top 100 in career HR

Points for:

Career Homers	— 1 for each 10 career homers
League Leads	—10 for lead, 5 for tie, 2.5 for four-way tie in 1981
Big Seasons	—30–39 HR = 10 pts., 40–49 = 20, 50–59 = 30, 60 or more = 40

N-Points—total of above three columns

Active Players in 1982 in Bold Face

	Player	Career HR/Rank	Points for: Career Homers	Points for: League Leads	Points for: Big Seasons	N Points
1.	Babe Ruth	714/2	71	110	290	471
2.	Hank Aaron	755/1	75	35	230	340
3.	Willie Mays	660/3	66	40	190	296
4.	Harmon Killebrew	573/5	57	50	180	287
5.	Jimmie Foxx	534/7	53	35	190	278
6.	Mickey Mantle	536/6	53	40	150	243
7.	Ralph Kiner	369/27	36	55	140	231
8.	Lou Gehrig	493/13	49	25	150	224
9.	Eddie Mathews	512/10tie	51	20	140	211
10.	Ernie Banks	512/10tie	51	20	120	191
11.	Frank Robinson	586/4	58	10	120	188
12.	Mel Ott	511/12	51	45	90	186
13.	**Mike Schmidt**	349/34	34	50	100	184
14.	Ted Williams	521/8tie	52	40	90	182
15.	Hank Greenberg	331/39	33	35	110	178

	Player	Career HR/Rank	Career Homers	League Leads	Big Seasons	N Points
				Points for:		
16.	Willie McCovey	521/8tie	52	25	90	167
17.	**Reggie Jackson**	464/16	46	25	90	161
18.	Duke Snider	407/19	40	10	110	160
19.	**Willie Stargell**	475/14tie	47	20	80	147
20.	Rocky Colavito	374/25	37	5	100	142
21.	Johnny Mize	359/30	35	35	70	140
22.	Frank Howard	382/21	38	20	80	138
23.	Joe DiMaggio	361/29	36	20	80	136
24.	Chuck Klein	300/47	30	35	60	125
	Richie Allen	351/33	35	20	70	125
26.	**Johnny Bench**	377/23tie	37	20	60	117
	Gil Hodges	370/26	37	0	80	117
28.	**Carl Yastrzemski**	442/17	44	10	60	114
	Hack Wilson	244/76	24	30	60	114
30.	Stan Musial	475/14tie	47	0	60	107
	Orlando Cepeda	379/22	37	10	60	107
32.	**George Foster**	261/63	26	20	60	106
33.	Hank Sauer	288/49tie	28	5	70	103
34.	**Dave Kingman**	329/40	32	20	50	102
	Billy Williams	426/18	42	0	60	102
36.	Roger Maris	275/57	27	10	60	97
	Norm Cash	377/23tie	37	0	60	97
38.	Bobby Bonds	332/38	33	0	60	93
39.	Rogers Hornsby	301/46	30	20	40	90
40.	Ted Kluszewski	279/55	27	10	50	87
41.	Cy Williams	251/70tie	25	30	30	85
42.	**Gorman Thomas**	197	19	15	50	84
43.	**Jim Rice**	237/83tie	23	20	40	83
44.	Rudy York	277/56	27	10	40	77
45.	Roy Campanella	242/77tie	24	0	50	74
	Ron Santo	342/35	34	0	40	74
47.	Gus Zernial	237/83tie	23	10	40	73
	Boog Powell	339/36	33	0	40	73
49.	Roy Sievers	318/42	31	10	30	71
50.	Al Rosen	192	19	20	30	69
51.	Gavvy Cravath	119	11	55	0	66
	Tony Perez	363/28	36	0	30	66
53.	**Lee May**	354/32	35	0	30	65
	Larry Doby	253/67tie	25	20	20	65
55.	Wally Berger	242/77tie	24	10	30	64
56.	Hal Trosky	228/89tie	22	0	40	62
	Dick Stuart	228/89tie	22	0	40	62
58.	**Graig Nettles**	313/44	31	10	20	61
59.	Al Simmons	307/45	30	0	30	60
60.	Jim Wynn	291/48	29	0	30	59
61.	Bob Johnson	288/49tie	28	0	30	58
	Frank Thomas	286/53	28	0	30	58

	Player	Career HR/Rank	Points for: Career Homers	Points for: League Leads	Points for: Big Seasons	N Points
63.	**Greg Luzinski**	262/62	26	0	30	56
64.	Bob Allison	256/64tie	25	0	30	55
	Yogi Berra	358/31	31	0	20	55
66.	**Ben Oglivie**	195	19	5	30	54
	Vern Stephens	247/73	24	10	20	54
68.	Joe Adcock	336/37	33	0	20	53
	Bill Nicholson	235/86	23	20	10	53
	Earl Averill	238/82	23	0	30	53
71.	George Scott	271/58	27	5	20	52
	Jeff Burroughs	222/94tie	22	0	30	52
73.	**Reggie Smith**	315/43	31	0	20	51
	Wally Post	210	21	0	30	51
75.	Charlie Keller	189	18	0	30	48
	Del Ennis	288/49tie	28	0	20	48
77.	Jim Gentile	179	17	0	30	47
	Harry Davis	75	7	40	0	47
79.	Tony Conigliaro	166	16	10	20	46
	Bill Melton	160	16	10	20	46
81.	**John Mayberry**	255/66	25	0	20	45
	Joe Gordon	253/67tie	25	0	20	45
83.	Frank Baker	96	9	35	0	44
	Deron Johnson	245/75	24	0	20	44
85.	**Bob Horner**	138	13	0	30	43
	Darrell Evans	232/88	23	0	20	43
	Dolph Camilli	239/81	23	10	10	43
88.	Johnny Callison	226/92	22	0	20	42
	Willie Horton	325/41	32	0	10	42
90.	**Don Baylor**	213	21	0	20	41
	Leon Wagner	211	21	0	20	41
	Rico Petrocelli	210	21	0	20	41
	Andy Pafko	213	21	0	20	41
94.	**Dave Winfield**	204	20	0	20	40
95.	Al Kaline	399/20	39	0	0	39
	Ken Williams	196	19	10	10	39
97.	**Eddie Murray**	165	16	2.5	20	38.5
98.	Ken Boyer	282/54	28	0	10	38
	Rusty Staub	287/52	28	0	10	38
100.	Nate Colbert	173	17	0	20	37
	Jim Hart	170	17	0	20	37

Other players in the top 100 in career homers, but not in the top 100 in N-points, Career HR/Rank:

Brooks Robinson, 268/59
Vic Wertz, 266/60
Bobby Thomson, 264/61
Vada Pinson, 256/64 tie
Joe Torre, 252/69
Bobby Murcer, 251/70 tie
Goose Goslin, 248/72
Joe Morgan, 246/74
Sal Bando, 242/77 tie
Roberto Clemente, 240/80

Gabby Hartnett, 236/85
Rick Monday, 234/87
Ron Cey, 228/89 tie
Bobby Doerr, 223/93
Ken Singleton, 222/94 tie
Tony Oliva, 220/96
Joe Pepitone, 219/97 tie
Jim Bottomley, 219/97 tie
Ron Fairly, 215/99
George Hendrick, 214/100

APPENDIX 3—Big Hitters (Baseball Personalities Named in This Book)

Aaron, Hank
Adcock, Joe
Aikens, Willie
Allen, Dick
Allison, Bob
Alou, Felipe
Anson, Cap
Appling, Luke
Armas, Tony
Averill, Earl (Sr.)
Bagby, Jim (Sr.)

Baker, Dusty
Baker, Frank
Bando, Sal
Banks, Ernie
Barlick, Al
Baylor, Don
Beck, Fred
Bell, Les
Bench, Johnny
Bender, Chief

Bentley, Jack
Berger, Wally
Berra, Yogi
Blackwell, Ewell
Blair, Paul
Blanchard, Johnny
Boggs, Wade
Bonds, Bobby
Bottomley, Jim
Boudreau, Lou
Boyer, Clete
Boyer, Ken
Brain, Dave
Branca, Ralph
Brett, George
Brett, Ken
Brock, Greg
Brock, Lou
Brooks, Hubie
Brown, Gates
Brown, Tommy
Bryant, Clay
Bunning, Jim
Burdette, Lou
Burns, Britt
Burgess, Smoky
Burroughs, Jeff
Butler, Brett
Byrne, Tommy
Callison, Johnny
Camilli, Dolph
Campanella, Roy
Campaneris, Bert
Campbell, Bruce
Carbo, Bernie
Carlton, Steve
Carter, Gary
Carty, Rico
Cash, Norm
Cavarretta, Phil
Cedeno, Cesar
Cepeda, Orlando

Cerone, Rick
Cerv, Bob
Cey, Ron
Chambliss, Chris
Clark, Jack
Clarke, Fred
Clarke, Nig
Clemente, Roberto
Clendenon, Donn
Clift, Harlond
Cloninger, Tony
Cobb, Ty
Colavito, Rocky
Colbert, Nate
Collins, Rip
Combs, Earle
Conigliaro, Tony
Connor, Roger
Cooper, Cecil
Cooper, Walker
Cooper, Wilbur
Covington, Wes
Cravath, Gavvy
Crawford, Pat
Crawford, Sam
Crawford, Willie
Cronin, Joe
Crowe, George
Cruz, Todd
Cuellar, Mike
Cullop, Nick
Cuyler, Kiki
Darwin, Bobby
Davis, Harry
Davis, Willie
DeCinces, Doug
Delahanty, Ed
Demaree, Frank
Dent, Bucky
Dickey, Bill
Dickson, Murry
DiMaggio, Joe

DiMaggio, Vince
Doby, Larry
Doerr, Bobby
Dougherty, Patsy
Doyle, Larry
Drysdale, Don
Dykes, Jimmy
Easter, Luke
Ennis, Del
Essegian, Chuck
Etten, Nick
Evans, Darrell
Evans, Dwight
Fairly, Ron
Feller, Bob
Ferrell, Rick
Ferrell, Wes
Fisk, Carlton
Foster, George
Fournier, Jack
Foxx, Jimmie
Frederick, Johnny
Freeman, Buck
Friberg, Barney
Gamble, Oscar
Garagiola, Joe
Gardner, Larry
Garvey, Steve
Gehrig, Lou
Gentile, Jim
Gibson, Bob
Gionfriddo, Al
Glenn, Joe
Goodman, Ival
Gordon, Joe
Goslin, Goose
Grant, Mudcat
Grantham, Boots
Greenberg, Hank
Grich, Bobby
Gross, Wayne
Guerrero, Pedro

Haas, Mule
Haines, Jesse
Hall, Jimmie
Harper, Tommy
Harrah, Toby
Harris, Bucky
Harris, Joe
Harrison, Roric
Hart, Jim
Hartnett, Gabby
Heep, Danny
Hendrick, George
Henrich, Tommy
Herman, Babe
Hernandez, Keith
Hernandez, Willie
Hickman, Piano Legs
Hiller, Chuck
Hobson, Butch
Hodges, Gil
Holmes, Tommy
Holtzman, Ken
Hooper, Harry
Horner, Bob
Hornsby, Rogers
Horton, Willie
Howard, Elston
Howard, Frank
Hubbell, Carl
Hunter, Catfish
Hurst, Don
Jackson, Joe
Jackson, Reggie
Jenkins, Ferguson
John, Tommy
Johnson, Bob
Johnson, Cliff
Johnson, Dave
Johnson, Deron
Johnson, Walter
Jones, Mack
Jones, Willie

Jordan, Tim
Jorgensen, Mike
Kaat, Jim
Kaline, Al
Kauff, Benny
Keeler, Willie
Keller, Charlie
Kelly, George
Kemp, Steve
Keough, Matt
Killebrew, Harmon
Killian, Ed
Kiner, Ralph
Kingman, Dave
Kittle, Ron
Klein, Chuck
Kluszewski, Ted
Kokos, Dick
Koufax, Sandy
Kranepool, Ed
Kreevich, Mike
Kuenn, Harvey
Kuhel, Joe
Kurowski, Whitey
Laabs, Chet
LaHoud, Joe
Lajoie, Nap
Landis, Kenesaw
Landreaux, Ken
Landrum, Tito
Larsen, Don
Lary, Lyn
Lavan, Doc
Lazzeri, Tony
Leach, Tommy
Lemon, Jim
Leonard, Dutch
Lolich, Mickey
Long, Dale
Lowe, Bobby
Luderus, Fred
Lumley, Harry

Luzinski, Greg
Lynch, Jerry
Lynn, Fred
Mack, Connie
MacPhail, Lee
Maddox, Garry
Magee, Sherry
Majeski, Hank
Mantle, Mickay
Maranville, Rabbit
Marberry, Firpo
Marichal, Juan
Maris, Roger
Marshall, Willard
Mason, Jim
Mathews, Eddie
Matthews, Gary
May, Lee
Mayberry, John
Mays, Willie
Mazeroski, Bill
McCarthy, Joe
McCarver, Tim
McCovey, Willie
McDougald, Gil
McGee, Willie
McGraw, John
McManus, Marty
McNally, Dave
McQuillan, Hugh
McRae, Hal
Medwick, Joe
Melton, Bill
Merkle, Fred
Meusel, Bob
Meusel, Irish
Meyer, Dan
Milner, Eddie
Mincher, Don
Miranda, Willie
Mize, John
Molitor, Paul

Monday, Rick
Moore, Eddie
Moreland, Keith
Morgan, Joe
Murcer, Bobby
Murphy, Dale
Murray, Eddie
Murray, Red
Musial, Stan
Nelson, Rocky
Nettles, Graig
Newcombe, Don
Nicholson, Bill
Nicholson, Dave
Niekro, Joe
Niekro, Phil
Nieman, Bob
Odwell, Fred
O'Doul, Lefty
Oglivie, Ben
Oliva, Tony
O'Neill, Mike
Otis, Amos
Ott, Mel
Pafko, Andy
Palmer, Jim
Parrish, Lance
Parrish, Larry
Patek, Freddie
Pepitone, Joe
Perez, Tony
Perry, Gaylord
Petrocelli, Rico
Pfeffer, Jeff
Piersall, Jimmy
Piniella, Lou
Pinson, Vada
Pipp, Wally
Post, Wally
Powell, Boog
Ramos, Pedro
Randolph, Willie

Redus, Gary
Reed, Jack
Rhodes, Dusty
Rice, Jim
Rice, Sam
Richard, J.R.
Richards, Paul
Richardson, Bobby
Rickey, Branch
Ripken, Cal
Roberts, Robin
Robertson, Bob
Robertson, Dave
Robinson, Brooks
Robinson, Frank
Robinson, Jackie
Roe, Preacher
Roenicke, Gary
Root, Charlie
Rosen, Al
Roth, Braggo
Rudi, Joe
Ruffing, Red
Ruth, Babe
Ryan, Nolan
Ryan, Rosy
Saier, Vic
Santiago, Jose
Santo, Ron
Sauer, Hank
Schmidt, Mike
Schoendienst, Red
Sconiers, Daryl
Scott, George
Schulte, Frank
Sebring, Jimmy
Seerey, Pat
Sewell, Rip
Seybold, Socks
Shamsky, Art
Sheckard, Jimmy
Sievers, Roy

Simmons, Al
Simmons, Curt
Simmons, Ted
Singleton, Ken
Sisler, Dick
Sisler, George
Skowron, Bill
Slaughter, Enos
Smalley, Roy III
Smith, Earl
Smith, Elmer
Smith, Reggie
Smith, Willie
Snider, Duke
Sothoron, Al
Spahn, Warren
Speaker, Tris
Spencer, Daryl
Stahl, Jake
Stargell, Willie
Staub, Rusty
Stngel, Casey
Stephens, Vern
Stobbs, Chuck
Stuart, Dick
Swoboda, Ron
Tenace, Gene
Thevenow, Tommy
Thomas, Frank
Thomas, Gorman
Thompson, Jason
Thomson, Bobby
Thornton, Andre
Tinker, Joe
Tobin, Jim
Torre, Joe
Trammell, Alan
Trosky, Hal
Upshaw, Willie

Vaughan, Arky
Veale, Bob
Vernon, Mickey
Wagner, Honus
Wagner, Leon
Walker, Tilly
Walsh, Ed
Walters, Bucky
Wambsganss, Bill
Waner, Lloyd
Waner , Paul
Ward, Aaron
Wertz, Vic
Whitaker, Lou
Whitfield, Fred
Wilhelm, Hoyt
Williams, Billy
Williams, Cy
Williams, Gus
Williams, Ken
Williams, Ted
Williamson, Ned
Wills, Bump
Wilson, Chief
Wilson, Hack
Wilson, Willie
Winfield, Dave
Wise, Rick
Wonka, Willie
Wynn, Early
Wynn, Jimmy
Yastrzemski, Carl
York, Rudy
Yount, Robin
Zabel, Zip
Zachary, Tom
Zernial, Gus
Zimmerman, Heinie
Zisk, Richie

ABOUT THE AUTHOR

A former newspaperman, Don Nelson's first love is writing, his second baseball. A member of the Society for American Baseball Research, he combines his talent in research and writing and his knowledge of baseball in this book. He grew up in Central Illinois. Don says: "I started following the Chicago Cubs when I was nine years old. I became a Cub fan. Home run hitter Bill Nicholson was one of my first heroes." Forty years later, he's still a loyal (and long suffering) Cub fan, but now works in Washington, D.C. and lives in a suburb of the Nation's Capital with his wife Mary and teenaged daughters Lee Ann and Cindy.